Man The Species: Almost Extinct

Man The Species: Almost Extinct

The Search for a New Paradigm

By Leonard E. Bellinson
As told to Mike MacCarthy

Writer's Showcase
San Jose New York Lincoln Shanghai

Man The Species: Almost Extinct
The Search for a New Paradigm

Writer's Showcase
an imprint of iUniverse.com, Inc.

For information address:
iUniverse.com, Inc.
5220 S 16th, Ste. 200
Lincoln, NE 68512
www.iuniverse.com

ISBN: 0-595-19210-6

Printed in the United States of America

This book is dedicated to Ellie, my wife and inspiration.

Contents

Preface

I consider this a societal health care book. I'm not a doctor nor am I a health care provider—by any stretch of the imagination. I've never worked in the field of medicine or psychology, nor am I what most of the world would call a scientist. By training, I'm a lawyer, businessman, and educator, but my passion has always been reading and writing. I consider my "extra-scientific" training an advantage for the reader because I'm not bound by the "politically correct" strictures usually associated with the academic community. Being an outsider allows me the freedom to question many of the basic assumptions of "so-called" scientists and reach my own conclusions without fear of professional alienation. My tenure is not at stake; I am free.

I am; therefore, I think. I like to examine the long view of things—trends I see developing in this country and around the world. That habit has always stood me in good stead, allowed me to see what was going to happen long before others—even helped me do reasonably well at making a living. But I'm retired now, my children are grown and there's no real reason for me to devote more energy and time to the acquisition of things;I have everything I'll ever need. So I look out across this blessed country and planet of ours and take mental notes of where we've been and where we're going.

When I look into the future 50 to 100 years and beyond, I see serious storm warnings not only for this country, but for all western civilization. I see mankind losing their way, and I see society as we know it falling into disarray. At the center of this chaos is the human male, or Man The Species (MTS) as I will refer to him. I need to be able to differentiate MTS from *Homo Sapiens* or the singular man in my discussions here, because all three play a significant role in the telling of this story. I want to emphasize for the reader that within these pages when I use MTS, I address that aspect of *Homo Sapiens* represented by the male. We will also talk at great length about the female, but the word "man" has many confusing meanings, which I hope to eliminate by the use of the acronym MTS.

Also, before plunging into the rest of the book, here are a few other definitions it would help for you to understand:

1. *Socio-biology* is my invented umbrella term for the whole cultural dynamic between men and women from a historical point of view.

2. *Neo-realism* goes back to the past, pulling out all that was good—music, philosophy, or art—bringing it into our lives and looking at its realistic value. It's taking an inventory of the historical aspects of culture that were of value, from a realistic standpoint, and trying to isolate genuine happiness from that realism rather than fantasies about it.

3. During your reading of this book, you will encounter various references to prehistoric time periods. For purposes of clarity, the following table presents generally accepted time periods for these various ages of prehistory in northwestern Europe (clearly there is a certain amount of overlap, but that's the way academia does things):

a. Paleolithic Period (Old Stone Age)	3,000,000 to 8,000 B. C.
b. Mesolithic Period (Middle Stone Age)	18,000 to 3,000 B. C.
c. Neolithic Period (New Stone Age)	3,000 to 1900 B. C.
d. Bronze Age	1,900 to 500 B. C.
e. Iron Age	500 to 51 B. C.

(publication of Julius Caesar's *Gallic Wars*)

Left alone to stumble through the emotional darkness caused by the dramatic changes in modern society of the past 150 years—especially the last 50—I see MTS thrashing about for answers to questions too many males have not bothered to ask. And, like the proverbial bull, I see him doing a lot of damage to himself as well as the rest of humankind in the process. The purpose of writing this book is to provide an "early warning" system for all of human civilization concerning the problems of MTS and society—the long-range problems.

However, before looking into the future, it seems appropriate to look into the ancient past so the reader can see what happened to MTS in true historical perspective and not just within the confines of the last 5,000 years—the centerpiece of our discussion. We will start our journey with a brief assessment of where we are, followed by acomprehensive overview of MTS going back to the beginning of time, and then work our way up to the Industrial Revolution. That represents a major turning point for MTS and his search to find a permanent and meaningful place in western civilization. MTS finally lost his way unlike any other time in human history. Why? Because since the middle nineteenth century, events have been happening too fast for civilization to really have time to reflect and examine things in historical perspective. It's been one war after another, one new major invention after another, one more new technological breakthrough after another. An essential element of this book will be to view the whole of history and especially that of *Homo Sapiens* from a more panoramic point of view than merely the past few hundred years or a few decades into the future.

Writing a book about the problems of the male is nothing *that* new; it's become a cottage industry in recent years. A long-range view into both our past and future will allow us to determine a new course. And that is new. After all, even though I'll be long gone when these problems become acute, I would hope that some of my readers agree with me and feel moved to advance other thoughtful long-range solutions for the future of the human male. However, from where I stand, if I fail to make my case convincingly and humankind does not insist on dramatic and systemic changes in the role MTS plays in society, the future for him and all of humanity looks bleak indeed.

Chapter One

Where Are We?

So you think I'm exaggerating about the deteriorating situation in modern civilization as it concerns the human male—how the fabric of our culture is crumbling before our unseeing eyes? You think I'm indulging in hyperbole when I assert that the United States male has allowed himself to become virtually useless in society and now teeters on the brink of extinction? What's the evidence? What do I see that makes me think there's such a crisis? Consider the following:

1. Roughly 50percent of all marriages now end in divorce;
2. The rates and numbers of children born to unwed mothers soar;
3. The number of female single-parent households is at an all-time high;
4. The cases of reported domestic violence are at an all-time high;
5. The number of men arrested for drug/alcohol abuse is at an all-time high
   (according to the Center for Disease Control, men's alcoholism exceeds women's by a ratio of 3:1 for all ages 15-44, 45-64, and 65 and above);
6. The number and percentage of men who are in jail is at an all-time high
   (men: 758,294; women: 46,230 =16:1 ratio);

7. The number of men who are committing suicide is skyrocketing;
8. Adolescent males are committing suicide at four times the rate of girls
   (15-19 is 4:1; 20-24 is 6:1);
9. Adolescent males are failing in school and dropping out at much higher rates and are increasingly less likely to go on to college;
10. The gap between the ages at which women and men die is widening (women now live longer than men by an average of eight years; in 1989 it was seven years).

No serious reader of the above historical data (there are more such facts, eachmore compelling) can deny there's a problem. The issue revolves around the meaning and significance of such statistical events. However, it's also important to remember that these facts are about people. When we say, for instance, that "the number of men who are committing suicide is skyrocketing," we're not talking about trees or chipmunks. We're talking about your father, my brother, her husband, a close friend's grandfather—real males who live next door, usher at your church, play at the same golf course, coach your child's ball team, work in the same building with you. And don't forget the young males still in high school or just going into the military or ready to graduate college or about to father their first child. They're real flesh and blood and all part of "Man The Species" (MTS).

And the news on this subject seems poised to get worse. During the next 100 years and beyond, western civilization—and the United States in particular—are going to experience more profound sociological changes involving the role of MTS. More women, not fewer, will be entering the workforce. More women, not fewer, will seek independence and shun the traditional institutions of marriage and family. More women, not fewer, will demand more choices. Having a man in their lives will become an option, not a necessity, for more and more adult women.

In addition, think ahead with me about some of the technological breakthroughs that are just on the horizon, all of which are going to have profound and shattering effects on society and especially further complicate the future role of MTS. Human cloning, the ability to surgically replace virtually every part of the human anatomy, an average life span of two hundred years, outer space travel, cold fusion, the manufacture of "intelligent" products, the development of gravitonics, and the harnessing of the power of antimatter which will eventually enable outer space travel at a much faster rate than the speed of light—not to mention a multitude of derivative applications.

When we ponder the numerous technological advances that have occurred within the past hundred years and extrapolate ahead to 2100 and beyond, it seems clear that unless MTS of western civilization pays close attention, he could easily soon find himself becoming as obsolete as yesterday's computers. Why? Because it's clear that society and the male in particular have forgotten one of the most important lessons of humankind's history—adapting to new environments. To this point in time, adaptability is the one attribute of *Homo Sapiens* that has enabled it to survive for approximately 3,500,000 years. Somehow, MTS has let that fact slip out of his consciousness. Let's take a few moments to quickly examine our historic ability to adapt to change.

When primates began to separate themselves from other mammals, three attributes eventually distinguished them for life in the trees: the development of forelimbs with delicate hands, a thumb; and the ability to grasp, hold, and manipulate objects. Because they could now live successfully in trees, their need to rely so heavily on their sense of smell diminished and their sense of sight became of primary importance. Over time, this caused their snouts to shrink to small nostrils and their eyes to grow enormously. Sight then became their most important sense because they had to locate food as if they were a bird without wings. These heightened visual faculties marked a new beginning for the expansion of their most important organ—the brain.

Over time, the larger apes climbed down to the ground and ultimately developed what we have to come to know as the heel on our lower extremities. This led to the first hominids who could walk in an upright position, thus freeing their forelimbs to be used in other and new ways. This meant that when they were particularly hungry, scavenging dead animal carcasses killed by dangerous predators became a new option. But due also to the rapid growth of their brain, their appetite for protein grew. Now what was once an option became a need. To regularly have access to meat, it became necessary for the early bipeds to scare off other scavengers such as vultures or hyenas. Throwing became a necessary skill and, with practice, enabled the killing of other mammals. This adaptive process is believed to have happened over a period of approximately a million years.

However, a diet largely composed of meat produced another problem—still larger brains. Increased brain size eventually meant longer childhoods, which resulted in new pressures on the female. No longer could she easily take care of herself and her child in the postpartum period. She required assistance that led to food sharing and the emergence of one of the first *socio-biological* contracts between the genders. Males had to kill and drag their prey back to the females and offspring for a communal meal. As meat consumption became a staple of their diet, the exchange of food for sex became a staple of life. Exacerbating this problem was the female's desperate physical need for iron that could only be found in meat. This event placed the male in a very strong negotiating position.

A further need for adaptation arose as a result of the rapid growth of the early hominoids' brain. The physical requirements of walking upright made it more and more difficult for the female to both meet her own needs and that of her offspring. Childbirth became increasingly traumatic due to the growing size of the head. Nature finally compensated by eliminating the major neuronal pathways for instinctual survival in most other mammals until after birth. The missing pieces would be supplied by what we now call culture. Other mammals such as geese, lions, and monkeys also learn elementary group behavior responses as they mature, but only in *Homo Sapiens* has culture taken on such an essential role. Human culture funnels its vital message into the brain of its offspring via a singularly unique medium—language.

This adaptation to the needs of environment worked to everyone's advantage then and continued to well serve the needs of hunter-gatherers during the intervening three million years. Up until approximately 5,000 years ago, the message from culture was fairly consistent as to the various roles of the male and female—one of cooperation; the *socio-biological* contract that has lasted the longest. But somewhere around 3,000 B.C., the roles of the male and female underwent a profound change—one that coincided with the approximate time of the invention of writing. With the advent of the written word, gender roles began a transformation that resulted in more and more power in the hands of the male and less and less available for the female. However, that societal aberration began to reverse itself about 150 years ago with the advent of the industrial revolution.

During this recent period since the beginning of industrial development, MTS has fought a losing battle to retain his power over the female and now, as we begin a new millennium, it's painfully obvious the old ways of MTS from 5,000 years ago no longer work. It's time for a new accommodation to environment—a new *socio-biological* contract, if you will—one without male domination. The big question is, how?

The answers can be found in history—always a valuable source when planning the future—but through a more in-depth review than just a few hundred years. The words of a famous philosopher seem appropriate here: "Those who cannot remember the past are condemned to repeat it." But in this case, maybe that's not such a bad idea. The threshold question seems to be: Which part of history would we like to repeat and which part would we be well advised to ignore?

Chapter Two

How Did We Get Here?

A. A Review of Pre-History's Societal Development

1. In The Beginning

Knowing what life was like before recorded history began is at best an inexact undertaking. Until the most recent quarter-century or so, mankind had little choice but to make "educated guesses" based on archeological finds from all over the world. However, with the invention of some of the new technology for testing the age of objects and our ability to analyze DNA from the most infinitesimal of materials, our confidence in the information we now have about our past seems quite reliable.

The history of *Homo Sapiens* actually began more than 600,000 years ago in Europe when fire is believed to have been discovered. At that time, virtually all human society could be characterized as belonging to the hunter-gatherer tribes, numbering about 100 people; each tribe freely roamed the face of the earth, taking care of each other, raising their children, and occasionally welcoming in an isolated outsider (usually a female). Such instances were exceptions, however; mostly, tribes simply interbred.

Somewhere in the ensuing half-million years, mankind confronted the finality of death and decided upon the concept of an afterlife. Extensive physical evidence exists of reverential burials and funeral rites going back 60,000-70,000 years, a defining characteristic in all human cultures ever since. There is also ample evidence that in these prehistoric civilizations, many myths came into widespread acceptance.

In *The Myth of the Goddess*, Anne Baring and Jules Cashford wrote, "The pregnant figures of the statues (pictured in their book) suggest that the myth of the mother goddess was concerned with the fertility and sacredness of life in all its aspects, and so with transformation and rebirth. By contrast, the myth of the hunter was concerned above all with the drama of survival—the taking of life as a ritual act in order to live. The first story is centered on the eternal image of the whole."

In many such cultures, a Great Mother Goddess held the twin powers of life and death. Recently, Joseph Campbell wrote: "So, from the Pyrenees to Lake Baikal, the evidence now is before us of a Late Stone Age mythology in which the outstanding single figure was the Naked Goddess. . . ." Even today among existing hunter-gatherer tribes, the concept of an all powerful Mother Goddess still lives and thrives and enables them to have great peace of mind. Campbell further opines: "The phases of the moon were the same for Old Stone Age man as they are for us; so also were the processes of the womb. It may therefore be that the initial observation that gave birth in the mind of man to a mythology of one mystery informing earthly and celestial things was the recognition of an accord between these two 'time-factored' orders: the celestial order of the waxing moon and the earthly order of the moon."

So one of the first things we know about prehistoric mankind was their reliance on goddesses as a way to explain their existence and afterlife. And without written words (at that time), all information and knowledge were passed on by the spoken word and retained by the use of memory. This arrangement produced a number of positive results for children as well as the entire society: There was a predictability about things—an order. Each tribe had three basic classes of people: elders, parents, and children. Eventually the youth grew up and became parents, then later became the elders. Each group knew their job, how they were supposed to do it, and who to ask if they had any questions. In relative terms, life was pretty simple for the hunter-gatherers.

But then along came the first truly traumatic cultural event that rocked the very foundations of the Stone Age *Homo Sapiens*. Later known in western civilization as agriculture, historians like to call it the herder-farmer period. How it happened, no one knows for a fact, but we can easily imagine. Someone noticed that seed scraps from the kitchen and abandoned in a compost pile would grow back the following season. From that it was easy to recognize the great potential benefits of intentionally planting seeds—a reliable food source. Mix in the discovery of animal husbandry and the wheel, and suddenly a new lifestyle begins to hold a stronger appeal. Why keep living as a nomad when one could remain in one place, keep his tribe safe, and when they were hungry, simply butcher one of the animals they had so carefully raised and kept in good health? This was much safer living and a lot better eating. Not only that, but the skills and knowledge of the hunter-gatherer tribe were easily transformed for farming. Growing crops out of the ground emphasized the feminine characteristics of both the male and female. Productivity and fruitfulness now moved to the forefront of the new society's value structure.

This proved an easy transition for females. Caring for young plants and livestock were nurturing tasks they had been performing all along in their role as mothers. Domestic animals, especially dogs, cats, and horses had been receiving scraps from the kitchen maiden since early Paleolithic times. At the dawn of history, all these animals had become established pets. The bond of love, a maternal principle, now extended beyond humans to other species.

For the males, the agricultural life was a huge adjustment. The daily "fight or flight" mentality had to be replaced by the notion of protection against other predators who wanted to eat *his* crops or steal *his* herds. Nevertheless, compared to the adrenaline rush hunter-gatherer males were accustomed to on a daily basis by possibly having to face a herd of charging bison, farming was a tame and boring existence. But with relative swiftness, these males converted their weapons of prey to tools of sustenance. In a historical sense, the speed with which this change took place could be categorized as a blink against the fullness of almost three million years. By the time the seventh millennium B.C. rolled around, agrarian communities had already begun to blossom throughout the Mediterranean and Southern Europe.

So in the transition from hunter-gatherer to herder-farmer (circa 7,000-10,000 years ago), we have a clear and concrete example of how the human male has undertaken a major social adjustment in the interests of the rest of civilization—specifically the women and children. Within a mere historical heartbeat, great numbers of nomadic tribes of approximately 100 people roaming the planet virtually disappeared.

2. Gender Motivation—The Prehistoric Paradigm

At this point, I would like to call attention to a cultural phenomenon I've decided to call the *seed carrier* compact. MTS is the medium for this event, and it is an essential component of the *socio-biological* contract between the male and female from all time. Woman is the receiver and nurturer of this seed—obvious stuff so far, right? However, the concept becomes infinitely more complicated when all of society accepts responsibility for the fulfillment of this compact. Now everyone is on the same team. It is my contention that this *seed carrier* agreement formed the heartbeat of the "what and why" of each gender's behavior in prehistoric society, and it is through an understanding of this process that I believe we will eventually unearth an acceptable solution for the future of our twenty-first century MTS. To every question there is an answer; the hard part is recognizing the answer when we find it.

No one knows exactly when it dawned on prehistoric mankind that not only did the act of procreation feel good, but it had several positive societal side effects—more able-bodied members to help with the work of survival, a bonding with other human beings as a result of shared experiences, someone to carry on the traditions and accumulated wisdoms of the tribe. And somewhere along the evolutionary timeline, the male noticed that the stronger he was, the more females seemed to make themselves available to carry his seed. And then after his transition from hunter-gatherer to herder-farmer, MTS noticed that a new paradigm had been established by females for their decision to make themselves available for seeding—territory. The more land he had or controlled, the more available females became.

From the female perspective, this changed paradigm made perfect sense. The more lands a herder-farmer commanded, the more nurturing elements—food, water, and the necessities of life—would be available to sustain her offspring. Her general nature was that of a nurturer to all life. Since she recognizes the basic need of MTS to plant his seed, she makes herself available to him when motivated to do so and sufficiently reassured. In the cultural system of the Mesolithic Period, males with lots of territory must have seemed like good potential partners.

Based on the most recent science, the accumulated historical evidence is compelling that this new herder-farmer society remained reasonably stable until approximately 7000-5000 B.C. The males still enjoyed access to many women; men and women worked in harmony to attend to the needs of their *tribes* (a tribe could number from several hundred to single digit); at the heart of that society was the Mother Earth Goddess. Males now came to embrace the belief that their own creation was the result of Mother Earth. Concerning those times, Historian Miraca Eliade wrote: "Woman and feminine sacredness are raised to the first rank. Since women played a decisive part in the domestication of plants, they become the owners of the cultivated fields, which raises their social position."

B. A History of the Goddess During Herder/Farmer Times

Prehistoric evidence is sketchy concerning exactly when important events occurred, but it seems that somewhere between 25,000 B.C. and 5,000 B. C., *Homo Sapiens* settled into a comfortable pattern of agrarian lifestyle. The males and females knew their roles, the general population could count on being fed, the children were being raised, and, from Europe to Siberia, a Mother Goddess sat at the center of all civilization. The women of this time period often held positions of importance in their different cultures and many became religious leaders for their respective communities. New research on old evidence further reveals that a considerable amount of the artwork found in caves throughout the world was created by female hands, and not by stereotypical men warriors who (as had been erroneously guessed by earlier so-called experts) were supposed to be depicting their emotions either before or after battle. In fact, the evidence is that it was the females who were in charge of these caves.

There are two important things to remember about this era: both males and females were content with their stations in life; there was a general sense of cooperation within those societies. [it was all they knew; they had to cooperate to survive] The empirical evidence supports the notion that once the transition from hunter-gatherer to herder-farmer had been made and sufficient time passed for this new lifestyle to settle in, there were few if any wars. At first, the various cultures had to find a way to absorb the need of MTS to "satisfy the hunter's craving for marrow sucked out of the splintered bones of fresh red kill," writes Leonard Shalan in his recent book *The Alphabet Versus The Goddess*. "The male's pent-up aggression," he continues, "began its toxic accumulation. Sport hunting, contests of courage, ritual killings, and human sacrifice came into being because of men's need to replace the excitement of the hunt." Despite these significant difficulties, MTS made the transition and eventually settlers located their villages in places where the soil was best for farming without regard to fortification against possible attack. Archeologists have discovered that the artifacts of such Mesolithic settlements contained a much more even distribution between domestic utensils and war weapons than would be the case after 5,000 B. C. Also, the artists who did their creative work on the walls of caves or at the gravesites depicted life without war or the male's domination of the female. Instead, women are shown holding positions of great importance, often much greater than that of the male. The burial sites from this period corroborate this picture of life for the herder-farmers of the late Stone Age. Most importantly, we now have a clearer picture of the religious framework during those times.

As we have noted earlier, the central figure of all sacred and cultural beliefs was the Earth Mother Goddess. She was responsible for life and death—symbolized during this period in artistic creations by showing all life and death coming from her womb. Nourishment came from her breasts and all Stone Age mankind considered themselves to be her children. However, the Mother Goddess manifested herself in many forms.

Throughout our discussion of this era, we've made repeated reference to the caves in which so much evidence has been discovered to help us understand our Mesolithic past. An essential point in our understanding of those times is the fact that caves were considered a most sacred place because they were believed to be the sanctuary of the Mother Goddess and the source of her regenerative powers. Only the most sacred members of those societies were allowed to enter. Excavations of sites at numerous locations around the world reveal "a continuity of life inside them over an immense span of time," state Baring and Cashford, ". . . for at least 20,000 years."

The entrances to these caves were quite impressive with their long, winding, and treacherous approaches and stunningly decorated walls. The pathways wound one to two miles from daylight into complete darkness deep in the bowels of the earth. The only lights these people had at their disposal were hollowed stones that held both burning oil from animal fat and juniper tree wicks. At the end of this path was a huge open, well-lit space. In 1926, Dr. Herbert Kuhn described one such site in France:

"The hall in which we are now standing is gigantic. We let the light of the lamps run along the ceiling and walls; a majestic room—and there, finally, are the pictures. From the top to bottom a whole wall is covered with engravings. The surface has been worked with tools of stone, and there we see marshaled the beasts that lived at the time in southern France: the mammoth, rhinoceros, bison, wild horse, bear, wild ass, reindeer, wolverine, musk ox; also the smaller animals appear: snowy owls, hares, and fish...And one sees darts everywhere, flying at game. Truly a picture of the hunt; the picture of the magic of the hunt."

Notice that that there were no pictures of battles or people fighting one another—simply pictures of men and women working in cooperation for the hunt. In many ways, this picture is reminiscent of what we in America witnessed in the past several hundred years when Native American tribes used to organize themselves for the hunt. This was especially made personal for many modern Americans in the movie *Dances With Wolves*. Also, there was a significance to the placing of the various paintings.

Baring and Cashford cite Andre Leroi-Gourham, "the pioneering French Palaeolithic scholar," who devoted a lifetime to the analysis of such sites. "What is fascinating is his observation that the figures, animals, and the signs he interpreted as feminine were situated at the central position, which was clearly 'the special heart and core of the caves.' The masculine animals and signs, by contrast, supplemented the feminine signs: either they were arranged around the feminine signs or they featured only peripherally in the narrow entrances towards the sanctuary or in the narrow tunnels at the back."

Another form the Mother Goddess assumed for Stone Age humans was that of a Bird. It was believed to be a messenger of wonder and a tangible manifestation of all that was invisible. In many cases the bird represented the weather or healing rain as well as water itself. In other places the bird carried a huge egg which some observers believe was a metaphor for the miraculous way beautiful life sprang from the Mother Goddess in much the same way a baby chick springs from an egg.

Another physical manifestation for the Mother Goddess was the moon. There are four phases of the moon: the waxing, the full, the waning, and the dark (the three days of darkness where the moon cannot be seen at all). Even today, mankind is fascinated by this dead planet poised out in space so close to our earth. We have the full benefit of knowing so much more about the moon by virtue of our scientific study and exploration especially during the 20th century. But our Palaeolithic brothers and sisters had no such advantage. As they stared up at this glowing circle of light, imagine their awe. Think how to them it must have appeared that a direct connection existed between the light and dark of the moon and the endless ebb and flow of the earth. How natural it must have been for them to see all life as being under her control and supervision; that everything they did had an effect on their relationship with Mother Goddess the moon. Consider the example of the 20th century scientist who traveled with the African Bushman (thought by many to be one of oldest races alive on earth today). One evening when he knew they had a long, tiring journey ahead of them the next day, the entire tribe danced all night to a waning moon. "We must show her," they told the scientist, "how we love her or she won't come back."

In 1963, according to Baring and Cashford, Alexander Marchack discovered that the Palaeolithic people used a system of lunar notation as far back as 40,000 B. C. "The tradition seems so widespread," Marchack wrote, "that the question arises as to whether its beginnings may not go back to the period of Neanderthal man—these facts are so new and important…they raise profound questions concerning the evolved intelligence and cognitive abilities of the human species."

Clearly, to prehistoric mankind, Mother moon was Mother of All. "She was the measure," writes Baring and Cashford, "of cycles of time, and of celestial and earthly connection and influence. She governed the fecundity of woman, the waters of the sea, and all the phases of increase and decrease. The seasons followed each other in sequence as the phases of the moon followed each other. She was an enduring image both of renewal in time and of a timeless totality, because what was apparently lost with the waning moon was restored with the waxing moon. Duality, imagined as the waxing and waning moon, was contained and transcended in her totality. So, analogously, life and earth did not have to be perceived as opposites, but could be seen as phases succeeding each other in a rhythm that was endless."

These are but just a few of the many physical manifestations the Mother Goddess assumed for the Palaeolithic and Neolithic peoples. But as the agrarian culture took root with all of *Homo Sapiens,* a new physical dimension for the Mother Goddess was about to permeate the late Stone Age mentality. Now she became responsible for the cycles of human and animal life, and those of the seasons, and of the agricultural year. The four phases of the moon now become embodied in the four seasons: spring is the waxing moon; summer is the full moon; fall is the waning moon; winter the dark moon.

Baring and Cashman explain these new developments thusly: "The secret source of life was still invisible: where the dark womb of the Palaeolithic Goddess had been the cave-temple, now it was hidden deep inside the earth. Human beings are still born from her, nourished by her and taken back by her. They sow the seed in her womb and harvest it as the substance of her body, transforming it themselves into bread. Plants, fruit, crops and animals that give milk, eggs, meat, wool and skins are all, like human beings, her children and are all, therefore, sacred.

"Moon, woman, earth—and the cycle of gestation in all three—can be seen to be governed by rhythm, order, and exact sequence of development. Woman, with the formation of the child in her womb tied to the precise time of ten [sic] months, continues to embody a sacrality that is possibly even more pronounced than it had been in the Palaeolithic. Campbell writes that woman 'participated—*perhaps even dominated* (emphasis added)—in the planting and reaping of the crops, and, as the mother of life and nourisher of life, was thought to assist the earth symbolically in its productivity."

As a result of this harmonious attitude toward life, great things began to happen in these societies. This information is fairly recent and has only come to light during the last quarter century. The new evidence shows that prior to 5,000 B. C., many of the settlements grew into communities of several thousand people. Pottery, stone-working, copper-working, the formation of rudimentary linear script all came to high levels of achievement during this time-frame. An excavation site in what used to be Yugoslavia (called Vinca) was once thought to have been developed by the Romans or Greeks; but, after recent radio-carbon testing, the true dates of the artifacts discovered there reveal that those spacious houses (some with two or three rooms—previously thought unheard of for those times) were built somewhere between 5300-4000 B. C.

The preponderance of all available evidence is that under the guidance of the Mother Goddess, mankind flourished during these times. According to Leonard Shlain, "In 1957, James Mellaart reported on his excavation of the earlier farming communities in southern Turkey, Catal Huyak and Hacilar, extant between 7,000 B. C. and 5,000 B. C. His and (Arthur) Evans's work broke new ground, forcing other archaeologists to reassess their views.

"Mellaart concluded that women had created Neolithic religion, developed agriculture, and controlled its products. He believed these factors explained the absence of military castes, central authority, and a science of warfare in Neolithic times. Archaeologists have not unearthed positive proof that Neolithic people ever fought organized wars."

Homo Sapiens seemed well on its way to establishing itself as a compassionate and noble species—one that lived in loving harmony with nature and itself.

So what went wrong? How did MTS get so far off track?

C. Why the Demise of the Goddess

1. The Turning Point

Next we will examine in detail what happened between 5,000 B. C. to 3,000 B. C.. The big question to be answered is: Why would humankind decide to change the herder/farmer civilizations that were—from all available evidence—operating at a high degree of satisfaction during most of this 2,000-year period?

There have been a number of theories. Some say it was the Kurgan warrior horseman of southern Russia who swept down upon the farming communities of the Mesopotamian and Old European alluvial plains and superimposed their own warrior mentality; others say it was the invention of the concept of private property that naturally followed as a result of the agrarian lifestyle; still other theories suggest the development of the idea of the ordered archaic state or even the notion of surplus wealth. Yet upon closer scrutiny, all these explanations fail to take into account the entire body of new evidence and understanding which (when studied) exposes the inconclusive nature of these arguments. Certainly each supposition played a role in the diminution of Goddesses, but none could objectively lay claim to having been the pivotal event.

Let's briefly review a summary chronology of significant world events immediately preceding and during that time period. According to Riane Eisler in her 1987 book *The Chalice & The Blade*, between 6,000 and 5,000 B. C., agricultural and food-producing economies spread across all of Europe; Catal Huyok flourished in Anatolia; rice flourished in Thailand; agrarian cultures developed in the Near East; copper metallurgy began in the middle Danube basin of Europe; the size of villages increased; and the use of sacred script emerged for use in religious cults.

Between 5,000 B. C. and 4,000 B. C., Old Europe (southwestern Europe) rose to cultural new heights: Ceramic art and architecture (two-story temple buildings) enjoyed new levels of excellence; unparalleled growth took place in the use of copper and gold, especially for use in trade; there was a wider use of vehicles drawn by horses; the colonization of the Mesopotamian plains took place; new agrarian settlements developed in Egypt; and Mexico adapted the cultivation of corn.

Between 4,000 B. C. and 3,000 B. C., even more startling events took place: Britain imported the Neolithic economy; early Megalithic monuments appeared in Brittany; the Chinese domesticated the moth; the Kurgans moved south from Russia into Mesopotamia and Old Europe, followed by marked changes in habitation patterns, social structure, economy, and religion; art from Old Europe dwindled to a mere trickle.

2. The Suspects

Clearly, several critical events took place during these two millennia (roughly the same time frame since the birth of Christ). It's equally obvious (from the above listing of events) Ms. Eisler believes the Kurgans are the villains in this historical detective story. However, according to author Leonard Shlain, the Kurgan explanation originated with Marija Gimbutas, an archaeologist, who "speculated in the 1960s that a semi-pastoral people called the Kurgan culture domesticated the horse in southern Russia around 5,000 B. C. and mounted the first cavalry. Gimbutas asserts that these horsemen swept down out of the steppes of Russia beginning in 4500 B. C. and fell upon peaceful agricultural settlements, killing the men, enslaving the women, and appropriating wealth and land. The Kurgan people, Gimbutas speculates, then repressed Earth Goddess worship, supplanting Her with their sky gods."

However, Dr. Shlain (in his book *The Alphabet Versus the Goddess: The Conflict Between Word and Image*, Penquin Putnam Books, 1998) argues that there are serious holes in the Kurgan explanation for the disappearance of the Goddess. "Wherever a primitive people have come in contact with a more sophisticated culture, the transmission of values has inevitably flowed from the advanced to the primitive. The Goddess people were more advanced than the pastoral Kurgan people. Agriculture has led the Goddess cultures to create permanent settlements, providing the stimuli for further economic diversification, and increasingly innovative progress in craft, metallurgy, invention, architecture, and knowledge.

"According to Gimbutas, the Kurgan herdsmen astutely appreciated the advantages of agricultural life and relinquished their nomadic ways, settling down to lord over the conquered farm folk. But since, by this act of imitation, they tacitly acknowledged the superiority of their vassals, why did not the Kurgan people pay homage to the Goddess? The theory that Kurgan horsemen dethroned the Goddess does not adequately explain the pervasive onset of the five-thousand-year reign of patriarchy."

So who were the Kurgans? Their name in Russian means "mound" and it refers to the way they buried their dead: in artificial mounds or barrows. As a people, little is known about them except that they were pastoralists (made their living by raising sheep) and breeders of horses. How it was that they came to adopt warrior and sky gods as the center of their culture remains a mystery to this day. Because they were nomads, roaming the vast wilderness, very little is known of their origins. Archaeologists have been unsuccessful in finding any concentration of their societies until they moved south and west. Why they moved and the derivation of the belief systems remain shrouded by a lack of information. Suffice it to say that without that knowledge, the evidence remains inconclusive as to whether or not the Kurgans are the major cause for mankind's decision to abandon the Goddess in favor of the invaders' harsh male gods. One fact that seems indisputable is that Kurgans did invade and after that, the Goddess began to fade.

Yet another contender for the title of "Destroyer of the Goddess Culture" could be the practice of *bride barter*. According to anthropologist Claude Lévi-Strauss, as his works have been characterized by author Leonard Shlan, "Inspired by the taboo against incest, *exogamy* served two purposes: it prevented the inherited congenital defects that occur with inbreeding and it strengthened inter-tribal alliances.…The tribe's elders more often exchanged their very young girls, rather than their older boys. Lévi-Strauss proposes that once men began to think of women as commodities, men began to appropriate women's power. His hypothesis does not explain the dramatic zigzag from masculine to feminine and then back to masculine principles that occurred before, during, and after the first five thousand years of agriculture. Why did most societies have such a strongly feminine orientation immediately after the arrival of agriculture, even though elders were still exchanging brides?"

Other authors such as Friedrich Engels, William Irwin Thompson, Jane Jacobs, and Gerda Lerner have proposed yet more theories. Engels seeks to blame the new concept of private property, but according to Shlain "ignores the possibility that males in hunter-gatherer societies also coveted property. In fact, nearly every male mammal, including our primate ancestors, exhibits intense feelings of territoriality." Thompson and Jacobs see the creation of surplus wealth as the agent of Goddess rejection; Lerner's supposition builds on that idea by stating that in order to "regulate trade, store surpluses, defend cities, and design irrigation projects, power necessarily became concentrated in the hands of a few." Thus was born the archaic state, armies, wars, and male domination. Shlain dismisses these concepts by observing: These hypotheses do not "account for the numerous Goddess-based archaic societies that were extant between seven thousand and five thousand years ago (5,000 to 3,000 B. C.). One has only to view the joyful murals at the palace of Knossos to appreciate the feminine nature of the Minoan culture. King Minos, the Greek myths tell us, demanded that other fiefdoms under his sway send healthy young slaves as tribute. If formation of archaic states brought patriarchy into being, then why were there many slave-owning Goddess-based archaic states in a period following the invention of agriculture but few after the beginning of recorded history?"

It seems fair to say that well-informed observers of these many possibilities do not agree as to one clear and proximate cause of the decline of Goddess-based societies. Author Shlain posits still one more theory of his own. "Rather than patriarchy resulting from an invasion from the *outside*, I propose that this radical shift from the feminine to the masculine, from the values of the caring mother to the ways of the domineering patriarch, was brought about by forces subtly at work on the *inside*. Something happened five thousand years ago that was as significant to its time as the discovery of agriculture had been five thousand years earlier to its age. It was not the Kurgan horsemen from the north who ended the reign of the Goddess, nor was it the creation of private property, nor surplus wealth. While these events may have played a role, I propose that the central factor in the fall of the Goddess was a revolutionary development which occurred during the same period—literacy. First writing, and then, its more sophisticated refinement, the alphabet, tolled the death knell of feminine values both metaphorically and, as we shall see, quite literally. Alphabets are the reason that Western culture's perception of reality radically shifted. This is literacy's hidden cost. The patriarchal warrior-dominator that plays so prominent a role in all Western history books succeeded *because of the invention of books themselves.*"

Many scoff when they hear this assertion. How can something that has brought so much hope, freedom, human and personal growth to the entire world be a vehicle of ignorance? Isn't that what we're talking about here—mankind's flight from an enlightened and cooperative culture to one of the patriarchal warrior-dominator? Isn't that what all major western and eastern civilizations have now become?

Because Shlain's theory is so new and hasn't been subjected to intense public scrutiny, it warrants more thoughtful analysis.

3. The Literacy Theory of Why the Goddess Disappeared: An Overview

According to the web site for *The Alphabet Versus the Goddess*, Leonard Shlain is "the author of *Art & Physics: Parallel Visions in Space, Time, and Light,* and a contributor to *The Encyclopedia of Creativity* (Academic Press, 1999) and *Stress and Survival*, edited by Charles Garfield. He has written for many publications and lectures widely.

Shlain is also Chief of Laparoscopic surgery at California-Pacific Medical Center in San Francisco and Associate Professor of Surgery at UCSF.

In the Preface to *The Alphabet Versus the Goddess*, Shlain writes, "By profession, I am a surgeon. I head a department at my medical center and I am an associate professor of surgery at a medical school. As a vascular surgeon operating on carotid arteries that supply blood to the brain, I have had the opportunity to observe firsthand the profoundly different functions by each of the brain's hemispheres. My unique perspective led me to propose a neuroanatomical hypothesis to explain why goddesses and priestesses disappeared from Western religions."

A neuroanatomical explanation for such an important anthropological question merits serious consideration. It would be so easy to simply dismiss his proposition out of hand because on its face it appears a heresy, but the fact that the author is an experienced witness to the working anatomy of the human brain gives me pause. The dynamics of a particular physical or mental act are of supreme importance to our discussion, so Dr. Shlain's observations hold immense potential for insights that would ordinarily be unavailable to such an anthropological investigation.

In the chapter that succeeds his announced theory, Shlain begins by explaining to his reader the mechanics of the brain during the act of reading and writing. "To speak," he begins, "we need the cooperation of both hemispheres of the brain, and we use *both* areas of the retina and we employ *both* hands."

However a more detailed explanation of the act of speech might be useful here. In a 1/24/00 article on the *Los Angeles Times* front page entitled "Scalpel, a Life, and Language," the newspaper's science editor Robert Lee Hotz writes, "Without a stumble, the average person can produce about 150 words a minute, each word selected in milliseconds from as many as 50,000 possibilities and arranged in a meaningful sequence dictated by an elaborate mental stylebook of grammar and syntax.

"So powerful is human language as an engine of thought that, by one computer estimate, it would take 10 trillion years just to speak all the possible sentences of no more 20 words.

"Armed with new insights into the cellular structure of thought, researchers are beginning to understand that the marriage of meaning—as expressed through language—and the human brain is far more intricate than anyone had imagined.

"The more complicated the grammar of a sentence, the larger the amount of brain tissue pressed into service, Carnegie Mellon University researchers have determined. The mental machinery of language triggers activity in both halves of the brain, whether words trip off the tongue or are signed on the hands, research shows. 'Language is a dynamo,' says neurolinguist Ursula Beluggi at the Salk Institute.

"No one knows just when the human species uttered its words or what triggered the evolution of its language ability, any more than individuals can recall that time in their lives before they learned to speak. Without words to give them substance, what form could such memories have?

"The archeological evidence—which is indirect at best—suggests that humanity acquired language about 500,000 years ago, according to anthropologist Leslie C. Aiello of the University of London. The fossil clues of primordial throats and jaws suggest that humanity's distinctive anatomical capacity for speech may have evolved some 2 million years ago.

"Men and women process language differently, brain imaging studies show. At Yale University, researchers Bennett and Sally Shaywitz found that language activity was concentrated in the brain's left hemisphere among men but occurred across both hemispheres in women."

It's important for our purposes that the reader take note of the fact that men and women are significantly different in how they process the act of speech and then store information in their brain.

Later in the next paragraph in his book, Shlain continues, "When written words began to supersede spoken words, the left brain's dominance markedly increased. To write **and** (emphasis added) read, an individual uses *primarily* the left hemisphere, *only* the hunting cones (the eyes) and *only* the killing hand (the dominant hand)." One page later he writes: "If the spoken word was the result of delicately balanced assignments of the feminine and the masculine sides of the brain, then the invention of writing completely upset this balance."

The concluding paragraph of Shlain's chapter named "Nonverbal/Verbal" reads: "The written word issues from *linearity, sequence, reductionism, abstraction, control, central vision,* and *the dominant hand*—all hunter/killer attributes. Writing represented a shift of tectonic proportions that fissured the integrated nature of gather/hunter communication and brain cooperation. Writing made the left brain, flanked by the incisive cones of the eye and the aggressive right hand, dominant over the right. The triumphant march of literacy that began 5,000 years ago conquered right-brain values, and, with them, the Goddess. Patriarchy and misogyny have been the inevitable result."

Author Shlain seems unusually sure of himself. Let's see if the facts bear him out that there is a direct correlation between where MTS finds himself today and the creation of the alphabet.

4. The Genesis of Patriarchy and Misogyny:

For reasons that are not immediately obvious, three events seem to have occurred almost simultaneously in the recorded history of *Homo Sapiens*: The invention of writing and reading; the development of patriarchy and the outbreak of serious killing wars between tribes; the onset of male gods at the expense of goddess.

Mankind's relentless march from the introduction of writing and reading down through the ensuing millennia of recorded history is filled with their male dominance, subjugation and enslavement of the female, the appearance of male gods, and the virtual disappearance of goddesses up to and including the 20th century. It is this 5,000-year flight into darkness and despair that is at the core of my thesis. Since (in relative terms) this period of time has been so short, there's no reason that mankind—and especially MTS—cannot reverse that process—or at least begin to reverse the process. But like any behavior modification, it must begin with a recognition of the problem.

At the heart of our discussion is the question, Why does MTS find himself almost incapable of conducting his affairs without violence? Is this a relatively *new* phenomenon or is it much older than what most "historians" would have us believe?

a. War:

There are two competing theories about war and the development of civilization. One assertion is that during those periods during which *Homo Sapiens* recognized the Goddess as its model for how society was to be run, war seldom occurred. The other and opposite proposition holds that war is a part of nature, rooted in our genes going back to our earliest ancestors and even before that.

In his book *The Dark Side of Man* (Helix Books, 1999), Michael P. Ghiglieri quotes from a report which appeared in *Geo Australia* entitled "Rock Art Warriors: World's Earliest Paintings of People at War."

"These Aboriginal paintings," the article states, "—dated at five thousand years ago and located in Kakadu, in Australia's Northern Territory—depicted men spearing one another in war. But contrary to the article's title, they were relatively recent. 'The earliest actual image of combat,' notes army intelligence analyst Robert L. O'Connell, 'a

Mesolithic cave painting [twenty thousand years old] at Morela la Vella in Spain, depicts men fighting with bows.' My point here is not to quibble about the oldest hard evidence of war. Instead it is to emphasize that wars are immensely older than even these paintings. As we will see, wars are older than humanity itself."

Ghiglieri then goes on to chronicle how closely related humans and chimpanzees are. "The recent discovery that chimps are the species most closely related to humans genetically (we share 98.4 percent of the same DNA)—and that we, not gorillas (they share 97.9 percent of the same DNA), are the species most closely related to chimps—makes the answer to this question (Why do chimps kill chimps?) significant.

"Today, due to decades of work in Gombe and Mahale Mountains Nationals Parks in Tazania, as well as shorter projects such as that by Christophe and Hewige Boesch in Tai National Park in Sierra Leone and mine and others' in Ugande Kibale National Park, we know more about chimps than any other wild non-human primate. And one thing we know is that the vital ingredient in the formula for chimp warfare is neither intelligence nor individuality nor the capacity to kill (although all of these play a role). Rather, it is their pattern of exogamy, the way genes transfer between groups.

"Unlike most social mammals, among whom the rule is for adult males to out-migrate to join a new group, male chimps never out-migrate. Only females do....This form of exogamy is rare. Of the more than two hundred species of primates known, we see male retention like this in fewer than ten—one of them being humans.

"Breaking this rule opens a Pandora's Box of cooperative male violence. As females emigrate and leave their brothers behind, the resulting community becomes a male kin group. This extended family of brothers, cousins, uncles and nephews, and fathers and sons shares so many genes that it sets the evolutionary stage for exotic male reproductive strategies based on cooperation, even in the face of death."

According to Ghiglieri, biologist William D. Hamilton inadvertently stumbled upon "one of the most important processes of natural selection: *kin selection,* when studying bees—"the process whereby family members increase the fitness of certain genes they carry by assisting one or more relatives to breed more than they otherwise would....The only chance sterile (bee) workers and soldiers have to reproduce their genes lies in their helping their mother to raise more queens—regardless of what that help costs them. This is because, by proxy, she and her queen progeny reproduce the very same genes the workers themselves carry. In short, reproductive slaves. The queen is *their* reproductive slave. Helping or defending her is, in fact, self-serving."

In response to Darwin's concept of "survival of the fittest", Ghiglieri pointed out that "*fittest* refers not to big muscles or marathon endurance or clever wits, but to the most reproductively successful genes. Secondarily, *fitness* refers to the fittest *individuals,* defined as those most successful reproductively." By way of clarification of the natural selection process, Ghiglieri further noted that "Hamilton coined the term *inclusive fitness* to define how one relative shares genetically when another breeds. For example. When my child reproduces, my genetic "share" of his or her success—the grandparent's coefficient of relatedness—is one-half of one-half, or one-quarter of a clone. Helping my grandchild yields half the genetic 'gain' in inclusive fitness as helping my child at the same age would. The concept of inclusive fitness reveals how a celibate uncle can paradoxically achieve high reproductive success by fostering the births of more nieces and nephews (whose coefficient of relatedness to him equals one-quarter) than his brothers and sisters otherwise would have raised.

"*Blood is thicker than water*" was dictated by inclusive fitness. In nature's arena, nepotism reigns supreme....Examples of human inclusive fitness could fill a library. Hunting-gathering peoples reveal some of the clearest examples. The Kung San of Kalahari, for example, shared the meat from their kills. Anthropology lecturers love to explain how beneficent these hunters were. What is rarely said, however, is that successful hunters shared first (sometimes only) with their families via very strict rules in which the closest relatives come first.

"'Me against my brother,' goes the old Arab proverb; 'me and my brother against my cousins; me, my brother, and my cousins against our non-relatives; me, my brother, cousins, and friends against our enemies in the village, all of these and the whole village against the next village.'

"If this proverb seems easy to understand, it is because inclusive behavior is so powerful in shaping our behavior—for good or evil. Inclusive fitness, for example, is the architect of nepotism, tribalism, nationalism, and racism, as well as of the tender mother-infant bond we admire. As biologist Richard Dawkins notes, William D. Hamilton's two papers on inclusive fitness in 1964 'are among the most important contributions to social ethology ever written.'

"No reasonable doubt exists today that the natural strategy of common chimpanzees is to establish, maintain, defend, or expand a kin group territory via lethal warfare....Now that we have seen the Machiavellian nature of martial chimpanzees, it is time to revisit *Homo sapiens*.

"Despite overwhelming evidence to the contrary, many recent books on war—*War* by Gwynne Dyer, *Aggression and War: Their Biological and Social Bases* by Jo Groebel and Robert A. Hinde, *On Killing: The Psychological Cost of Learning to Kill in War and Society* by Dave Grossman, *Of Arms and Men* by Robert L. O'Connell, and *Blood Rites* by Barabara Ehrenreich—insist, in unabashed wishful thinking, that killing is an acquired proclivity that society must inculcate into men. Men, they say, do not possess an instinct to kill other men, because that would be bad for the species. These books all were written by people who understood little or no biology—or who simply ignored or denied its findings.

"The central 'truth' of sociologists is that nature, especially that of humankind, is nice and that people are designed to do things that, all in all, favor the survival of their species. Hence, people could never be equipped by nature with instincts to kill other people. This idea comes from the Bambi school of biology, a Disneyesque vision of nature as a collection of moralistic and altruistic creatures. It admires nature for its harmony and beauty of form and for its apparent "balance" or even cooperativeness. It admires the deer for its beauty and fleetness, and it grudgingly admires the lion for its power and nobility of form. If anything is really wrong with us, it explains, it is *socio*-cultural problem that we can fix by re-socializing people. It is not a biological problem.

"Nature, however, is actually a dynamic state of recurring strife—of relentless competition, dedicated predators and parasites, and selfish defense....Since the first pair of amoebas vied over a tidbit of organic detritus, conflict has been in nature. [Author] Robert L. O'Connell explains:

> Weapons are truly ancient, far older than man—perhaps nearly as old as life itself. It is among the stingers of colonial invertebrates and the body armor of Paleozoic crustaceans that the genesis of weaponry is to be found....Too frequently, weapons development is viewed as fundamentally unnatural, a particular curse of mankind that sets him at cross-purposes with the mechanisms of his environment. This is far from true. The world of nature is essentially a violent one.

Ghiglieri then goes on to point out, "This violent world of nature, including human nature, multiplied by millions of competing species, is one that biology has revealed to us." But he wonders later in the same chapter, "Why War?"—then advances his own solution.

"The answer lies in male versus female biology. Due to the endless reproductive contest between men, and due to how much less men must invest in children compared to what women do, sexual selection and kin selection have designed human males—compelled human males—to wage war as a strategy to cooperatively seize the territory, resources, and women of other men and to use them reproductively. Indeed, when in 1993 cognitive psychologist Leda Cosmides posed the question, 'Why would anyone be so stupid as to initiate a war?' the data were so clear that they allowed her to answer it with no oversimplification, '*To get women*.'

"*War is typically men's ultimate reproductive gamble. Many researchers agree that the goal most worth the lethal risk of war is women or the resources that attract or support more women and their offspring.* That *something* men—or male apes—seek through war is selfishly expanding or securing their own families."

b. The Seed-Carrier Concept:

A male perspective:

One of the basic premises of this book has to do with an insight that assigns to MTS a *socio*-biological attribute I choose to call "seed carrier." It's consistent with what Ghiglieri has said earlier, and I'm therefore identifying with MTS who arrives on this planet with the ability to think and look around and realize that the earth is part of some comet. He sees some part of this infinite number of stars and that this earth is in an orbit with a sun and moon. And, for some reason, that relationship between the earth and the sun creates a protoplasm which works on the earth's minerals with enough water to create a different form of animated sediment called mankind of which MTS represents only half (approximately) of its total population. So he quickly comes to the conclusion that he cannot achieve his most basic needs by himself, the most compelling of which is the need to procreate.

MTS also observes that Mother Nature is committed to the male sperm fertilizing the female eggs in most species including humans, but which gender carries the offspring to term could be a subject of further research in the distant future. (**Note:** An interesting and unusual anomaly of nature is that the sea horse male—according to the *Encyclopedia Britannica*—"not the female, carries the fertilized eggs. The eggs, deposited in a brood pouch beneath the male's tail by the female, remain there until they hatch. At that time, the male contorts his body and expels the young through the single opening in the pouch.") Meanwhile, though, MTS must reach an accommodation with the other half of *Homo Sapiens*—Woman—in order to give his life meaning. She is the Mother Earth of his seed, and in order to plant more "seed," MTS recognizes that he needs more "lands" or women.

As Ghiglieri has also already written, the human "seed carrier" needs more physical territory, control over "the production" of the territory, power and control of the fertilizing of his seed. The more he fertilizes: the better he's maintained; the better he's able to plant, and the better he's able to nourish and harvest his fields. Over the many millennia since 70,000 or 100,000 B.C., this has never changed—whether he's a hunter-gatherer or a farmer or a city-dweller living in different countries, states, cities, villages, tribes, neighborhoods. In the end, males are enslaved by the need to "plant their seed."

The essential quality of MTS in this scheme of things is that he carry the seed in order to procreate and then, with enhanced reproductive options, have the knowledge and awareness of how to strengthen his seed. But society doesn't call it that. We call it doing well in the world; we call it education and achieving—the essence of which is that, as seed-planters, males also have to follow the example of farmers—find healthy earth that will be receptive to his seed; fertilize, water, nourish, and prepare the soil; and then finally, plant the seed.

I believe that most of the things men do—earning a living, trying to be knowledgeable, courting, etc.—are all different parts of the same motivation: seed planting. The song "You Don't Bring Me Flowers Anymore" suggests that flowers were bought and courting took place to make the earth (the woman) more receptive to the seeding. Jewelry, clothes, potential for a good lifestyle, physical attractiveness and strength sometimes work to make MTS more acceptable to Woman Earth.

But after he's planted his seed, the ardency of MTS's interest in that particular soil recedes. Of course, human society knows that the male wants to keep planting and there are many other "fields" in which to plant his seed, but the ardor for a particular "field" after each planting experience quickly ebbs. Soon, MTS runs out of "fields" and finds himself losing most of his function, other than to go back and "replant his fields" or strengthen his seed by adding new fields.

The history of civilization is filled with such activities; they're called war, arms build-up and preparedness, high-stakes military or industrial espionage, annexation or colonization, acquisition through victory in battle, piracy and high seas adventure, politics, treasure hunting, dueling, or exploring dangerous or forbidden frontiers. Many or most of these activities have been and continue to be outlawed or have fallen out of vogue, yet from a physiological and seed-strengthening point of view—*socio*-biological, if you will—they're entirely appropriate.

For MTS this attitude of disapproval and rejection by the other half of society produces high feelings of anxiety and loneliness within males. "We're just doing what comes naturally," they announce with little conviction, "why doesn't anyone understand? It's not personal, it's simply the humanity of MTS; it's not personal, it's just the genes, ladies and gentlemen—just the genes. This is just our nature—natural seed strengthening. Period. It's been that way through all recorded history?"

Yet to most females (and a growing number of males) such activity and attitudes are now unacceptable. "What about the use of intelligence and self-discipline to regulate appetites in the name of the common good?" they ask. "Surely the male *Homo Sapiens* has evolved further than just beyond the mentality of his chimp brothers."

A basic divergence based on differences in the *socio-biological* nature of men and women establishes the front line of the confusion for a good deal of modern society.

A female perspective:

The other half of this "seed-carrier" polarity is Woman The Species (WTS), and I call her the *seed nurturer*. The male wants and needs WTS to strengthen his seed—to think he's powerful, valuable, important. These are all things that have to do with seed strengthening. Before he feels it is safe to plant his seed in a particular "field," he must be convinced that this woman is attracted by his seed planting ability and the strength of his seed—the chemistry or alchemy of their union. (Note: The word alchemy comes from medieval Latin, from the Arabic "alchemia" which comes from the Greek word "chumeia," an ancient metallurgical term having to do with pouring. A similar sounding Chinese word meant "sperm of gold." There has also been a suggestion that alchemy comes from ancient Egypt as well as Arabic Hebrew.)

WTS, on the other hand, in a *socio-biological* sense, feels very much like the field or "Mother Earth." Ideally, she would like a male—who is like the good farmer—to plant his seed and take care of his fields by maintaining them in harmony with nature through proper nourishment and care. But just like the soil and the rest of planet earth, experience teaches her to have several contingency plans against the thoughtless and irresponsible farmer who doesn't prepare or take care of his fields.

In the final analysis, WTS must insure that the harvest—the baby— receives the necessary nurturing, caring, food and shelter, and unconditional love. She receives the sperm, combines the egg of the earth with his seed and, through her natural bodily functions, nourishes the seed to a full harvest. And long after the physical pain of that experience passes, she continues her historic role as chief *nourisher* of the child. (**Note:** The reader should not interpret this section as an endorsement or agreement by me with this sort of irresponsible behavior by males. I merely wish to chronicle what I see as a historically accurate picture of the role the different genders have played in this socio-biological drama we call human society.) Meanwhile, the male felt free to go back and strengthen his seed. Until recent times (the last 50 years or so), the dominant motivation for MTS was where he could next sow his seeds.

c. The Seed-Carrier Co-Conspirators

But without his fellow conspirators (during the past 5,000 years), MTS would have been unable to implement this giant hoax. Since all the males tacitly agreed to embrace this so-called new "truth" of male superiority (read patriarchy), WTS found themselves unable to create significant breaks the male ranks. After all, why would any "red-blooded" male be so foolish as to publicly admit that in the long run patriarchy was a self-destructive concept? Society under those terms so heavily favored them.

But what was the connecting tissue that bound vast numbers of seed carriers together? The continuous enjoyment of seed-mating lasts only a few seconds. It's interesting to note how nice grain looks in the grain seed, the enjoyment of like seeds jostling together as one. Men stand more alone like one seed—separate—while deriving strength from the independence of the seed planting, yet males can and do work together. As a consequence, MTS developed hunting groups, business groups, social groups, and the like—to create better nourishment for the seeds of the whole.

On the other hand, many males see the folly of a patriarchal society, but their ineffectual minority voice is most often drowned out by the roar of their *status quo* brethren. Is rock and roll the scream of the primitive seed-carrier crying out to be let loose from this out-moded form of civilization—to be set free? Are these males a wild seed driven away by the wind of a male-dominated culture because they seek another path toward connectiveness?

Women relate through their connectiveness—mater, grandmother, the tactile experience of plunging their callused hands deep into the moist soil. Women have typically worked together to nourish the earth without competition and aggression against other groups of women. However, feminine intimacy has nothing to do with the goal of seed-strengthening or power, but has everything to do with harmony—balance with Mother Earth—a togetherness, an inter-connectedness with those who need to be nourished. Most nourishers—not all, but most—are women and they work to help, heal, and care for the children *and* each other.

d. Monotheism and the Seed-Carrier

One of the all-time great enigmas and problems for people on earth is that the Hebrews discovered the concept of Yahweh, the one God. From that came Christianity and then for 2,000 years we have a vile, unceremonious break between the Jews and the Christians. The Jewish/Hebrew Yahweh was a very strict God. He talked about morality and responsibility. And He talked about man's responsibility—how MTS in a patriarchal society should live, and the rules for all society under this system. Judaism then led to Christianity, but other religions didn't talk about the essential part of seed strengthening—the perennialism of the seed. When you fully consider the real message of Christianity, it offers man the seed of "perennialness." He dies, goes into the ground, and, through Christ, can be born again. The evidence that he had a very good seed—the kind that goes into the earth and comes back—was and remains extremely compelling. An important nuance behind the Judo/Christian belief system was that it was one of the first monotheistic cultures to recognize the essential need of man to come back from death. Buddhism offers somewhat the same thing but lacks the conviction that we will come back as humans. Islam suggests that its seed is the strongest seed and conversion should be accomplished by force if necessary, which was also true of the early Israelites.

Christianity, Judaism, and Buddhism teach the concept of the ultimate seed strengthening and have, therefore, maintained their appeal to huge numbers of people through the ages. Their believers are strong enough to live, die, and live again while the essential biological and physiological fact is that the woman carries the baby, the man plants the seed in the woman, and, for all intents and purposes, retires from the scene.

The human embryo then becomes part of WTS; she centers her life around its nurturement. Ultimately, the baby comes and becomes part of her and her nature. This life-giving source is dedicated to the maintenance of the child—the caring, nurturing, providing shelter which also includes decorating, protection, and involvement. Later, she will teach her offspring what roots to eat, how to rest, and how to defend themselves. A different kind of interdependence with that child than what most males have been later trained to do by society or by the great monotheistic faiths—especially before the birth of Christ. The appearance on the world scene of the great monotheistic faiths seems to follow as an answer to the ancient great empires which took it upon themselves to overrun the known world with their armies, their murder, their pillage and rape, their enslavement, their mis-use of women.

So why would anyone be so stupid as to initiate a war? *To get women.* Why not? That's what society expected of MTS…. Right? And besides, MTS had more seeds that needed planting. Until Christ, monotheism (in general terms) was just another rallying cry for new armies to defeat armies who believed in polytheism. The notion of war wasn't new, but replacing the Mother Goddess in the major cultures of the world with male gods—or, in the case of monotheistic societies, one male god—was new. More importantly, almost none of these male gods questioned the concept of war. War and religion remained virtually one and the same until the 30th year of one highly unusual man's life. But how did it happen that in so short a period (in historical terms) that the Mother Goddess had been completely replaced?

5. The Vanishing Goddess—A Historical Review

Now that we've examined some of the factors that were responsible for the beginning of the demise of the Goddess between 5,000 B. C. to 3,000 B. C., let's briefly overview the history of the Goddess from 3,000 B.C. until modern times. This is an essential component of our journey to understanding the problems of where MTS finds himself at the dawn of the third millenium AD. A firm grasp of this time period and its significance for the Goddess will form the backbone of a startling new insight into the root causes of the disappearance of female deities.

To make this overview journey, we must begin with the so-called Bronze Age which is generally agreed by historians to have occurred from 3,500 B.C. until 1,250 B.C. This period in the history of humankind is so-named not because of the discovery of Bronze, but because of the military implications of this new metallurgical amalgam.

Bronze is an alloy of copper and tin. Its invention permitted more flexible and durable implements for use in the rapidly expanding herder/farmer communities throughout Europe, Asia Minor, the Near, and Middle East. But for those males who had war on their minds, this new technology was like a miracle: Weapons made of bronze were not only lighter in weight, but they also wouldn't break during combat. That meant that no longer did generals have to worry about replacing the broken battle-axes or swords or shields of their men in the heat of battle; now their soldiers had to simply concentrate on holding onto their weapons.

Because of another invention of this period—writing—historians can now trace the history of the goddess through the stories of those times on their architecture, tablets of clay, and strips of papyrus. Now the Mother Goddess of the Paleolithic and Neolithic times had become the Primordial Goddess and had family. No longer did she represent only the "whole" spiritual world, now she and her family were simultaneously "parts" of that dimension as well. This time was the beginning of a profound re-definition of humankind's understanding of the intricacy of its deity icons to themselves, each other, and their relationship to all life on earth.

According to authors Baring and Cashford, "The pattern of this story may have been inspired by humanity's relationship to the moon. For countless thousands of years human beings had seen the light growing to fullness, then giving way to the darkness and being reborn from it again and again in a continuous rhythm that must have felt eternal. In the Paleolithic era the moon gave people time: sequence, duration, and recurrence. In the Neolithic, the cycles of the moon were experienced in the cycle of the crops, where the light and dark phases of the moon were reflected in the fertile and barren phases of the earth. Now, in the Bronze Age, the moon's phases were given dramatic form in the great myths that have come down to us from Mesopotamia, Egypt, Anatolia, Syria, and Greece. They become a story that is lived by goddess and gods in their changing relations to each other and to humanity on earth.

"The moon was an image in the sky that was always changing yet was always the same. What endured was the cycle, whose totality could never be seen at any one moment. All that was visible was the constant interplay between light and dark in an ever-recurring sequence. Implicitly, however, the early people must have come to see every part of the cycle from the perspective of the whole. The individual phases could not be named, nor the relation between them expressed, without assuming the presence of the whole cycle. The whole was indivisible, an enduring and unchanging circle, yet it contained the visible phases.

Symbolically, it was as if the visible 'came from' and 'returned to' the invisible—like being born and dying, and being born again."

Much later, the Greeks assigned names to these two parts of the spiritual world, according to Baring and Cashford: "Relating this to the moon, *zoe* becomes the totality of the cycle of the moon's phases, and *bios* becomes the individual phases....The Great Mother Goddess can be recognized as the totality of the lunar cycle—as *zoe*—and her daughter and son-lover, who emerges from and return to her, can be seen as the moon's phases—as *bios*. Together they image the two 'faces' of life: eternal and transitory, unmanifest and manifest, invisible and visible. The son and daughter personify the ever-dying and ever-renewed forms of life, whether human, animal, or plant. Related to the cycles of the earth's seasons, the son and daughter incarnate the life of vegetation. The transitional moments in the agricultural cycle are commemorated with festivals of mourning and rejoicing, and in the great mythic dramas that express the mysterious analogy between the life of the moon, the life of the plants, and the life of the human beings. Participating in these rituals created a trust that as darkness is always followed by light, so death is followed by rebirth. All life, therefore, holds a promise of renewal. The sacred marriage, in which the mother goddess as bride is united with her son as lover, reconnects symbolically the two 'worlds' of *zoe* and *bios*, and it is this union that regenerates the earth."

During this same general era, another unprecedented event shook the foundations of the then known world—the discovery of knowledge by the priesthood: writing, mathematics, and astronomy. Baring and Cashford quote the author Joseph Campbell: "Towering temples symbolic of a new image of the universe made their appearance at the time—the first examples of monumental architecture in the history of civilization; and it is within the precincts of those sanctuaries that the members of a new type of highly specialized, heaven-gazing priesthood invented , *ca* 3200 B.C., writing, mathematical notation (both sexagesimal and decimal), and the beginnings of a true science of exact astronomical observation…This life-transfiguring concept of a celestial based political and social order reached Egypt *ca* 2850 B.C. with the founding of the First Dynasty; Crete on the one hand, India on the other, *ca* 2500 B.C."

Baring and Cashford then add, "The images of the constellations, the months of the year, the hours and seconds that still mark the passage of time in the twentieth century are the inheritance of the Sumerian discoveries some 5,500 years ago."

Another event of great social moment in terms of the demise of the Mother Goddess during the Bronze Age was humankind's push to live in closer proximity than ever before. With greater community knowledge came food surpluses and population groupings such as priests, farmers, craftsmen, and a new category of society—warriors. Also, because of the constant threat of invasion, communities had to be organized for the common defense. Baring and Cashford write: "Instead of villages clustered around a temple-mound and focused on agriculture and pastoral activities, there is the city, and then the city-state ruled by a king, who had increasingly to use his powers to defend his land. The temple was no longer the concern of the headman of the village but of a body of priests, who also organized the life of the community and were responsible for keeping accounts, taxation, apportioning land, and distributing food. In Sumeria the movement from the countryside to the city became irreversible, as the population was continually threatened by attack."

This new social order led to the gradual diminution of the Mother Goddess and the ascendancy of father gods. At first, all manner of human activity came to be governed by a god or goddess to whom all would turn for help or guidance during moments of strife or joy. Soon "Mother" and "Father" deities produced offspring and an intricate "family" tree developed to explain the various inter-family relationships. Gradually, the Father God began to assume a more central role while the other gods and goddesses receded to the background. This produced (among other results) deities of the earth and sky which were separated by the God of Air.

In Egypt and Sumeria, historians and archeologists discovered the first record of the myths of the disconnect between Earth and Heaven. Baring and Cashford write: "The separation of heaven and earth is an image of the birth of consciousness in which humanity is set apart from nature. The self who perceives and values is separated from that which is perceived and evaluated. Creation myths that show the division of the primal unity into two halves portray the human capacity to act reflectively rather than instinctively, which inevitably involves an initial disassociation from the instinctive life of nature. This new development of consciousness finds expression in the god who orders from beyond rather than the goddess who orders from within. The difficulty of this dissociation is the temptation to call the goddess (nature) 'lower' and the god (spirit) 'higher', assuming that consciousness can evolve only through making the distinction between what is wanted and what is not wanted, striving to reach the one and avoid the other."

This new thinking produces an inclination toward more conflict between various individual members of the deity family—gods and goddesses. As a result, there's more confusion and no simple solution by the various players. Enter the "hero." Baring and Cashford explain: "Here the ancient hunting instinct is diverted away from the animal to the new demands of survival. The heroic action of the gifted individual was needed in every sphere of life, and the heroic individual becomes the 'forerunner of mankind in general', as Neumann says, defining the task that will eventually have to be accomplished by all individuals. The appearance of the myth of the hero shifts the focus of attention from the great round of nature, expressed as the myth of the goddess, to 'the world as the center of the universe, the spot upon which man stands'. It is possible to see what we referred to as myth of the hunter in the Paleolithic age has now become the myth of the hero."

a. Invasions of the Migratory Warriors

Now another significant historical event occurs. The Kurgan invasions that had their genesis in Europe during the fifth millennium B.C. now begin to affect the rest of the known world. Joseph Campbell writes: "Towards the close of the Age of Bronze and, more strongly, with the dawn of the Iron Age (*c.* 1250 B.C. in the Levant), the old cosmology and mythology of the goddess mother were radically transformed, reinterpreted, and in large measure even suppressed, by those suddenly intrusive patriarchal warrior tribesmen whose traditions have come down to us chiefly in the Old and New Testaments and in the myths of Greece. Two extensive geographical matrices were the source lands of these insurgent warrior waves: for the Semites, the Syro-Arabian deserts, where as ranging nomads, they herded sheep and goats and later mastered the camel, and, for the Hellenic-Aryan stems, the broad plains of Europe and south Russia, where they had grazed their herds of cattle and mastered the horse."

Campbell is the master of understatement. Baring and Cashford provide a more graphic picture of the bloody holocaust: "Wherever they (the patriarchal warrior tribesmen) penetrated, they established themselves as the ruling caste and their appearance is marked by a trail of devastation: in Anatolia alone some 300 cities were sacked and burned, among them Troy (*c.* 2300 B.C.), and this pattern was repeated from Greece to the Indus Valley. There is little trace of the goddess myth to mitigate the barbarism of this ethos or reunite the parts set in opposition to each other, a situation of conflict that has endured to the present day. The echo of the mythology of war, which resounds in the *Mahabharata* as it does in the *Illiad* and the Old Testament, descends from these Bronze Age migrations.

"As a result of the Aryan and Semitic invasions, attitudes to life and to death were radically altered, as life was experienced as untrustworthy, and violent death became the norm rather then the exception. A relationship with nature many thousands of years old was disrupted as people no longer felt safe in villages, and sought refuge first in towns and then in cities girded by immense walls. A new social group—that of the warrior—came into being and the former close-knit group of farmers became little more than serfs. Indeed, the whole character of the mythology changes as the goddess as well as gods are infected by the warrior ethos, ratifying the barbaric actions of kings whose territorial ambitions draw them ever more deeply into the compulsion to conquer and enslave other peoples."

As a direct result of these cataclysmic political and military events, the social fabric of virtually all society was ripped from its historic moorings. Once again, Joseph Campbell puts things into perspective. "It is now perfectly clear," he writes, "that before the violent entry of the late Bronze Age and early Iron Age nomadic Aryan cattle-herders from the north and Semitic sheep-and-goat-herders from the south into the cult sites of the ancient world, there had prevailed in that world an essentially organic, vegetal, non-heroic view of the nature and necessities of life that was completely repugnant to these lion hearts for whom not the patient toil of earth but the battle spear and its plunder were the source of both wealth and joy. In the older mother myths and rites the light and darker aspects of the mixed thing that is life had been honored equally together, whereas in the later, male-orientated, patriarchal myths, all that is good and noble was attributed to the new, heroic master gods, leaving to the native nature powers the character only of darkness—to which, also, a negative moral judgment now was added. For, as a great body of evidence shows, the social as well as mythic orders of the two contrasting ways of life were opposed. Where the goddess had been venerated as the giver and supporter of life as well as consumer of the dead, women as her representatives had been accorded a paramount position in society as well as in cult. Such an order of female-dominated social and cultic custom is termed, in a broad and general way, the order of Mother Right. And opposed to such, without quarter, is the order of the Patriarchy, with an ardor of righteous eloquence and a fury of fire and sword."

b. The End of Mother Right

Previously, from the dawn of humankind, the order of "Mother Right" had held sway throughout most cultures. Indeed, the Mother Right was still at heart of most of the world's cultures well into the Bronze Age. Baring and Cashford tell us, "In early Sumeria, as in early Egypt and Crete, women played a public role in society, particularly the priestesses. They owned property, transacted business, and their interests were protected in the law courts. Sisters and brothers inherited property on equal terms from the family estate. Daughters who married took a dowry with them, which they kept in the event of divorce. In the centuries after 2300 B.C. the status of women in Sumerian society deteriorated. Although they still owned property, their husbands had to be consulted before buying and selling. Concurrently with these changes, the female deities in the Sumerian pantheon also lost their former position.

"Moreover, in the Akkadian north of Sumeria, which later became known as Babylonia, the Semitic tribes regarded women as possessions of men. Fathers and husbands claimed the power of life and death over daughters and wives. Sons inherited from their fathers and brothers. The birth of a son was hailed as a blessing, while the daughter could be exposed to die. Although the Semitic state of Babylonia ratified, in Hammurabi's famous code (1800 B.C.), the earlier Sumerian laws relating to the position of women, there is a marked deterioration after the third millennium B.C., which suggests the strengthening of the Semitic over the Sumerian attitude. This was given added impetus by the customs of the Aryan people, who had no priestesses and treated women as servants or chattels."

Thus were born attitudes and customs which (with few historical aberrations) continued uninterrupted until the end of the 19th century and finally gained complete public rejection by the end of the 20th century (at least in the United States)—a total span of some 3,700 years. When seen in the context of the fullness of all time, 3,700 years is a mere statistical blip. When viewed in human terms, it is one of the most stark examples of mankind's inhumanity to itself. In terms of MTS, it is truly one of his darkest hours.

However, the journey of misogyny and patriarchy from 1,800 B.C. to 2,000 A.D. has not been one continuous path of male misuse of his fellow female. There have been important deviations that are worth taking a moment to more closely examine.

c. A Significant Aberration

The Old Testament forms the cultural backbone of the Judeo/Islamic/Christian ethic which currently comprises approximately 60 percent of the world's population. It therefore seems appropriate to investigate what (if any) role goddess may have played in the creation of the document itself or in the lives of the men and women whose lives form the raw material of its message.

The first thing we should remember is that there is no word for goddess in the Hebrew language. The second thing we should bear in mind is that because the goddess played such an important role in the Sumerian, Babylonian, and Egyptian cultures, the goddess tradition was an intricate part of who those people were. According to Baring and Cashford, "[Yet] when disaster struck Israel, as when the ten tribes of the northern province were dispersed throughout the Assyrian Empire, or when the captivity in Babylon was imposed on the people of Judah, the fault was found in the regression of the Hebrews to the Canaanite religion. Responsibility was laid at the feet of the goddess, but why? Did the people then worship a goddess before they were converted to the religion of the monotheistic Yahweh? One interesting point of this story is that, even after the Exile, as much as half the population of Palestine did not participate in orthodox Judaism. It was these people—the poorer sections of the community, who had been deported to Babylon—who actually continued in the old beliefs and, as Halevi writes, 'limited and threatened the legalistic vision of the priests'.

"Many passages in the Old Testament that refer to Yahweh's anger against foreign gods are perplexing if the existence of shrines, temples, and statues of the goddess is not taken into account. When the Hebrews entered Canaan, they did not find a sparsely populated land with primitive people, but a country with a powerful religion and cultural tradition in which queens took the role of high priestesses, and ordinary women were priestesses. Strong and wealthy cities had long been established in Canaan that had trading connections with Egypt, Babylonia, and the Hittite kingdom in Anatolia. Canaanite rulers had often married princesses from these foreign courts, and the early Hebrews kings followed this tradition."

Raphael Patai in his 1990 book *The Hebrew Goddess* writes how the goddess played a major role in the lives of these people "from the conquest of Canaan to the Babylonian Exile." Then, according to Baring and Cashford, she disappears for about 1,500 years when, "the goddess image subtly reappears in the medieval Kabbalistic literature of the Jewish communities in Spain and south-western France as the Shekhinah and as the Matronit: the Matron, Lady or Queen. Conceived as intercessor between humanity and the deity, she is related, in this role, to the Christian Mary. Patai writes:

"'In view of the general human, psychologically determined predisposition to believe in and worship goddesses, it would be strange if the Hebrew-Jewish religion, which flourished for centuries in a region of intensive goddess cults, had remained immune to them. Yet this is precisely the picture one gets when one views Hebrew religion through the polarizing prisms of Mosaic legislation and prophetic teaching. God, this view maintains, revealed Himself in successive stages to Adam, Noah, Abraham, Isaac, and Jacob, and gave his law to Moses on

Mount Sinai. Biblical religion, in this perspective, is universal ethical monotheism, cast in ritual-legal form.

"'Historical scrutiny, however, shows that for many centuries following the traditional date of Sinaitic revelation, this religion, idealized in retrospect, remained a demand rather than a fact. Further study indicates that there were among the Biblical Hebrews other religious trends, powerful in their attraction for the common people and their leaders alike, in which the worship of goddesses played as important a role as it did anywhere else in comparable stages of religious development.'"

It should therefore come as no surprise to the reader that, according to Baring and Cashford, "In Moses, the chosen leader of the Hebrews, a residual and symbolic form of the old myth of the goddess and her son-lover still survives, despite its transformation by the Hebrew priesthood." Moreover, they explain, "The relationship of the patriarchs Abraham and Joseph to their wives, as well as the relationship of David to Bath-sheba and of Solomon to his royal Egyptian bride, suggests a deep memory of the mythological relationship between the pharaoh as Osiris and his sister-wife Isis. This theme has been explored by Edmund Leech in his discussion of the relationship of Moses to his sister, Miriam. The fact that there may have been a tradition that recognized the goddess in the mother and sister of Moses is implied in the third-century-AD mural in a synagogue at Dura Europos in Syria; Moses as an infant is shown as having emerged from a sarcophagus, held in the arms of a woman whose nakedness (in contrast to all the other female figures) suggests that she is a goddess.

"Patai believes that this is the image of the Jewish Shekhinah, who is first mentioned by this name in the first century A.D. The Shekhinah was known variously as the manifest, or 'presence', of Yahweh, as the bride of Yahweh, or as the Holy Spirit—the intercessor and binding link between the divine and human dimensions....In the earlier Talmudic and Midrashic sources this idea is implicit in the saying that, of all men,

Moses was the only one to whom the Shekhinah spoke 'every hour without setting a time in advance', and that, therefore, in order to be always in a state of ritual purity to receive a communication from the Shekhinah, Moses separated himself completely from his wife.

"Nonetheless, the banished imagery of the goddess mysteriously reappears, but now displaced and disguised in a new and unlikely context: as the people of Israel. Somehow, presumably unconsciously, the former mythological image was re-created."

It is against this backdrop that the powerful drama we have come know as the Old Testament played out and was recorded by its various authors—all the while ignoring the presence of the many goddesses of the world around them. However, there was another goddess-like presence the sacred scribes could not dismiss—the cherubim. Angels. Patai goes into great detail detailing many cherubim of the Old Testament—those in the Garden of Eden; the cherubim of the Ark; the cherubim of the Holy of Holies, reflecting "the union of Yahweh with the Community of Israel, his bride."

But in the New Testament we witness the most important deviation from the historical male obsession to denigrate the goddess. Baring and Cashford write, "Central to Christian doctrine from the fourth century AD was the teaching that as Christ was the second Adam, so Mary was the 'Second Eve', that Mary through her virginity had redeemed the sin of Eve. The paradise that had been lost was now regained, since the transmission of original sin had been finally interrupted by the untainted birth of Christ.

"Mary is the unrecognized Mother Goddess of the Christian tradition. Apart from the first chapter of Luke, where she holds the center of the stage in the story of the Annunciation, Mary appears very infrequently in the Gospels, and then she plays a completely subordinate role to her son. Yet within 500 years of her "death" a pantheon of images enveloped her until she assumed the presence and stature of all the goddess before her—Cybele, Aphrodite, Demeter, Astatrte, Isis, Hathor, Inanna, and Ishtar."

Joseph Campbell sees Mary this way: "It is simply a fact—deal with it as you will—that the mythology of the dead and resurrected god has been known for millenniums to the neolithic and post-neolithic Levant...The entire ancient world, from Asia Minor to the Nile and from Greece to the Indus Valley, abounds in figurines of the naked female form, in various attitudes of the all-supporting, all-including goddess...And so it came to pass that, in the end and to our day, Mary, Queen of Martyrs, became the sole inheritor of all the names and forms, sorrows, joys, and consolations of the goddess-mother in the Western World: Seat of Wisdom...Vessel of Honor...Mystical Rose...House of Gold...Gate of Heaven...Morning Star...Refuge of sinners...Queen of Angels...Queen of Peace."

As we overview the development of the cultures of the world—especially the development of western civilization—it is painfully clear that with few exceptions (the Virgin Mary being one) since 5,000 B.C., MTS has gone out of his way to systematically and methodically exterminate the notion of the goddess. Yet despite these determined efforts, female deities are now (2000 A.D.) beginning to get a second look from anthropologists and sociological prognosticators. However, before we fully examine that phenomenon, we should first examine in greater detail one unconscious cause of why MTS may have come to systematically destroy the concept of goddess. That moving force was the discovery of the *written word*.

d. Language/Writing/Reading—Pre-Industrial Revolution

d1. Introduction

It's ironic. In their award-winning book, *The Myth of the Goddess,* Baring and Cashford, while writing on a completely different subject, made the following insightful observation: "Yet the momentous discovery of the Bronze Age was the art of writing [not the discovery of bronze or its implications in terms of war, which the authors were then reporting]." For them it was *momentous* because now they could find records to aid them in their search for the truth about the Great Mother Goddess. But for author Leonard Shlain, his story was just beginning.

When last we discussed *The Alphabet Versus The Goddess,* our investigation into the mechanics of the brain while writing had just concluded. Shlain told us: "Writing made the left brain, flanked by the incisive cones of the eye and the aggressive right hand, dominant over the right. The triumphant march of literacy that began 5,000 years ago conquered right-brain values, and, with them, the Goddess. Patriarchy and misogyny have been the inevitable result."

We have now completed a brief overview of the history of the Goddess up through the Industrial Revolution and the second millenium. It's appropriate that we do the same for the profound influence of writing—it's that important in the history of humankind. Shlain quotes Joseph Brodsky to underscore this very point: "In the history of *Homo sapiens,* the book is an anthropological development, similar essentially to the invention of the wheel." The history of MTS, the rise and fall of the Goddess, and writing—most especially the alphabet—are inextricably intertwined. You'll see what I mean.

d2. The Beginning of Writing: The Sumerians & Egyptians

In the beginning there were pictures. Pictures were the only media besides speech, and the pictures appeared everywhere humans settled and developed a community. Petroglyphs were the only record left by our Stone Age brothers and sisters. Then around 3000 B.C., things began to change. The agriculture societies of the Fertile Crescent—Mesopotamia and Egypt—began to develop their own distinctive forms of writing.

According to Shlain [throughout this section about the inter-relationship between the alphabet and the fall of the Goddess, anything in quotation marks is from his book, *The Alphabet Versus The Goddess*], "The first Mesopotamians were Sumerians, a loose federation of communities on the rich plain between the Tigris and Euphrates Rivers. The Sumerians' irrigation system led to bountiful harvests and burgeoning towns. The twin settlements of Uruk and Ur became large enough to be called cities. As commerce expanded, the thorny problems of keeping track of transactions (sheep for barley, oats for goats) created the need for better recorded keeping. In devising a solution, the Sumerians took the first step in a process that would reconfigure all human realtions. By gouging tiny wedge-shaped marks with sharp sticks into wet clay tablets, they invented the first written language. Beginning in 3100 B.C., the first cuneiform figures appeared."

Five hundred years later, the Akkadians conquered the Sumerians and then improved the cuneiform system. By about 2300 B.C. it was written left to right, but by specially trained scribes who made it their life's work and memorized the large number of characters. Gradually, these scribes supplanted the elders and shamans and little by little gods became changed from female to male. The male scribes saw to it that there were written laws and they became the interpreters of these laws. "One-fourth of the code relates to women's rights, or more accurately, restrictions on women's rights....The first Mesopotamian written law code, *ca* 2350 B.C. [was] 'If a woman speaks out against her man, her mouth shall be crushed with a hot brick.'"

Meanwhile Egypt was growing up out of the Nile River Valley of Northern Africa. Around 3000 B.C. a pictorial script appeared in their culture which we now call hieroglyphs; this marked the beginning of their civilization. "Though based on images, Egyptian script was more than a sophisticated form of picture-writing. Each picture/glyph served three functions: (1) to represent the image of a thing or action, (2) to stand for the sound of a syllable, and (3) to clarify the precise meaning of adjoining glyphs. Writing hieroglyphs required some artistic skill, limiting the number chosen to learn it.

"While hieroglyphs were able to express most ideas, some concepts presented a challenge for a language based on pictures. To solve this problem, the Egyptians invented twenty-five icons to represent each of their language's spoken consonants and thus allow the reader to sound out a word-concept anacrostically. This is the principle of the alphabet. Although the Egyptian scribes had developed the first rudimentary alphabet, they used this new shorthand sparingly. They failed to recognize how useful and economical a small number of signs corresponding to the individual phonemes of their spoken language could be."

Between the Sumerians and the Egyptians, the Goddess faired best in the culture of the latter well into the Egyptian Middle Kingdom (2040-1600 B.C.). It was at this point that literacy became more firmly established, and the "female deities" began to lose "their preeminence." Then in the so-called New Kingdom (1550-700 B.C.), a new script began to take the place of the classical hieroglyphs; it was called *hieratic script* and "relied on the principle of phonetic pronunciation." It also involved changing from vertical to horizontal writing. With these changes came an even stronger outbreak of patriarchy. "In every society that learned the written word, the female deity lost ground to the male deity. Before the invention of writing, these two powerful forces had remained entwined in sexual union. In every Mediterranean society that embraced literacy, women lost their hold and fell from grace—economically, politically, and spiritually....The most dramatic changes for women were yet to come; the coming storm was brewing in the lands between Mesopotamia and Egypt."

d3. The Israelites/Hebrews & the Alphabet

We now turn to author Eric Haveloc for an additional insight into the importance of writing in the history of all humankind:

> "It is only as language is written down that it becomes possible to think about it. The acoustic medium, being incapable of visualization, did not achieve recognition as a phenomenon wholly separable from the person who used it. But in the alphabetized document the medium became objectified. There it was, reproduced perfectly in the alphabet...no longer just a function of "me" the speaker, but a document with an independent existence."

In the first two thousand years after the beginnings of Mesopotamia and Egypt groups of herders wandered the lands now bounded by "present-day Israel, Jordan, Lebanon, Syria, and the Sinai Peninsula. [They] would all have sunk into obscurity except for one stunning discovery. Someone, or some group among them, invented a greatly simplified method of written communication that shifted the perceptual mode by which people understood their reality, deflected the thrust of gender politics, and changed the course of history. This new scrivening was the alphabet. [according to the Encyclopedia Britannica: *In the early Hyksos period—17th century B.C.—the Northwestern Semites living in Egypt adapted hieroglyphic characters—in at least two differing forms of letter—to their own purposes. Thus was developed the earliest known purely consonantal alphabet, imitated in northern Syria, with the addition of two letters to designate vowels used with the glottal catch. This alphabet spread rapidly and was in quite common use among* the Northwestern Semites (Canaanites, Hebrews, Aramaeans, and especially the Phoenicians) soon after its invention. By the 9th century B.C. the Phoenicians were using it in the western Mediterranean, and the Greeks and Phrygians adopted it in the 8th.]

"What made the alphabet so revolutionary was the ease with which people could learn it. Because it was in their interest to keep others ignorant, the scribes of Egypt and Mesopotamia guarded the secrets of the written word. One who was literate had an immense advantage over those who were not, whether they were powerful or poor.

"The alphabet ended the hegemony of the literate elite. Instead of a complex syllabary of over 600 cuneiform characters, or 6,000 hieroglyphs with rules of grammar that would daunt the most eager student, an alphabet contained a mere twenty-odd letters [*An alphabet by definition is any form of writing that contains fewer than 30 signs*]. Thus an empowering skill that had been guarded by a favored few was now accessible to the multitudes. The religions that henceforth spiraled outward from unwinding reams of written scrolls demanded that acolytes be literate. Until that time, to know the deity one had only to *see* Her image or observe Her rituals. With the advent of the alphabet, to know the deity demanded that one first **read** His written words."

The question of which civilization actually discovered the alphabet is one that has never been proven beyond any shadow of doubt, but several facts concerning that issue are worth noting for our purposes. "Most archaeologists acknowledge that the oldest alphabet discovered is the one in the Sinai desert. In 1905, Sir William Flinders Petrie found a script resembling Hebrew letters at the site of an Egyptian temple dedicated to a goddess. Surrounding the area were rocks upon which Petrie found further evidence of this alphabet. Petrie called these precursor letters, dated around 1800 B.C., the Proto-sinaitic alphabet. Few challenge the fact that the sinaitic inscriptions are the oldest known alphabet script....There is only one major event associated with the name 'Sinai.' It was here that Yahweh gave Moses the Ten

Commandments for the Hebrew people. It seems like an extraordinary coincidence and a striking intersection of myth and science that the oldest alphabet was found in *the* place where the seminal episode in the history of the ancient Hebrew occurred."

The Hebrew people are thus thought to be responsible for the promulgation and dissemination of three pivotal ideas in the history of humankind: the alphabet, monotheism, and ". . . a code of morality that stands above human intercourse. The Ten Commandments applied *universally* to everyone. No king, pharaoh, or potentate was above the law. If human society was to be organized on a principle other than 'might makes right,' all would have to submit. The codes of Draco, Solon, and Justinian, the Magna Carta, the United States Constitution, and the Miranda rights can all be traced back to what happened in the Sinai.

But the question remains, "how did a landless, powerless, nomadic people, wandering in a dusty, rock-strewn environment, come to…such ideas by themselves? The key is that Yahweh expected all His chosen people to *read* what He had written.…He sanctioned only written words. It is not mere coincidence that the first *book* (emphasis added) written in an alphabet is the Old Testament. There is none earlier."

More importantly, for the reader, the genesis of the disappearance of the Goddess now rears its first sprout.

*   *   *

For Jews, the most important section of the Old Testament is the Torah—the first five books. According to the most recent research, "The oldest sections of the Torah were first transcribed between 1,000 and 900 B.C., and subsequently underwent three major revisions, with the later sections added over the next millennium…The Hebrews were older than the Greeks; the Old Testament is older than the *Iliad.* Moses was not only a great lawgiver and champion of Yahweh, he appears to have been the first word-smith." Shlain proposes that it was [the Hebrews] who bequeathed the alphabet to the Canaanites, who taught it to the Phoenicians, who then transmitted it to the Greeks.

The Romans copied the Greeks: "In the turmoil following the fall of Judea to the Romans around the time of Christ, rabbis, desperately trying to preserve Jewish identity, refused to sanction any further revisions in the Old Testament. But new generations needed to reinterpret the Scriptures in light of new situations, and scholars subsequently added rich compendia to the original document. The most familiar of these post-Diaspora writings is the Talmud.

"In A.D. 367, Christians canonized the New Testament, acknowledging the ancient book of the Hebrews as an integral part of their own story. Subsequently, the Muslims did so too. The Old Testament's triad of monotheism, Rule by Law, and the command to live ethically eventually became universal Western values."

In this brief summary, we have before us an overview of the first 2,000 years or so of the written word. Yet within this historical summary lies the unfortunate tale of the fall from cultural grace of the Goddess and the simultaneous increased suffering of the female at the hands of these male-dominated societies. Apparently, having a male deity, Rule by Law, and ethical living did not include the concept of equality; that would have to come later—much later. We will now re-trace the gradual demise of the Goddess during these two millennia, in parallel with the development of the alphabet. This journey in-detail will prove essential when we later address the question of a potential solution to the dilemma MTS presently faces.

d4. *The Alphabet and the Greeks*

As we learned earlier, the Goddess was an integral part of Egyptian society well into the Egyptian Middle Kingdom (2040-1600 B.C.). It was at this point that literacy became more firmly established, and "female deities" began to lose "their preeminence." Shlain points out that "Israel and Greece were the first two cultures that unreservedly embraced the alphabet."

In our discussions, we've briefly reviewed early Jewish culture, but little about the Greeks. According to modern research and technology, the Phoenicians first exposed the alphabet to the Greeks. Their alphabet was difficult for the Greeks to read because of a lack of precision with respect to pronunciation. So they decided to improve the alphabet by creating seven new letters to represent vowel sounds and decreasing the number of letters to 24. These few changes made it possible for the Greek people to enjoy high rates of literacy. However, included in that literary tradition were the great books the *Iliad* and *Theognis*. "The death throes of the Great Mother can be read between the lines of these sexist credos.

"When Homer transcribed the *Iliad* into alphabetic script in the eighth century B.C.," the author continues "a distinct oral Greek culture had existed for seven hundred years. During that time, Greeks worshipped a plethora of deities, each of whom exemplified specific traits of human behavior. In addition to the Olympian Golden Circle of twelve key deities, their pantheon included myriad naiads, satyrs, and nymphs, all of whom engaged in convoluted adventures and inventive liaisons. Out of this divine crush the Greeks wove a grand mythological tapestry.

"Yet, despite this protean variety, after the introduction of the alphabet, the Greeks lamented that Mount Olympus was short one god embodying one type of behavior. The Greeks broke the golden circle in the fifth century B.C. and ejected Hestia, goddess of the hearth, family, and children. Her replacement was Dionysus, god of wine, sexuality, and dance. The missing behavior was madness. The dynamic growth of his cult coincided with the rise of alphabet literacy, Greek rationality, and the flowering of classical art."

It also signaled the beginning of the rise of patriarchy which is clear in the evolution of the Dionysus persona. His birth involved seven months gestation in his mother (Semele who had been impregnated by Zeus) who Zeus, in a fit of anger and revenge, then set on fire. "Seeing her once fair form burned and disfigured," Shalin explains, "Zeus, experiencing an uncharacteristic surge of remorse, split open her pregnant belly and snatched the fetus, Dionysus, who had narrowly survived this maternal conflagration.

"Summoning Hermes, the god of trickery, Zeus had the fetus sewn under the skin of his groin in close proximity to the royal genitals swaying gently above the fetus's inguinal cocoon. These unusual neighbors would strongly influence the essential character of Dionysus. When the full nine months were up, Dionysus was born…again. The Greeks would call him the 'twice born' or the 'born again.' As with the birth of Hera, Athena, and Aphrodite, a male arrogated the female's most central function."

Not only was the birth of Dionysus laced with patriarchal metaphors, but so was "the boy-god's" public manifestations. Cursed by Hera (Mrs. Zeus) with occasional madness, "It seems more than coincidence that the Greeks, who codified logic, would at the same time elevate madness to a place of honor. Dionysus (madness) and Appollo (reason) alternated in presiding over the sacred oracle of Delphi (One tradition states that Delphi became Apollo's shrine after he usurped it from its original goddess, Themis. According to Plutarch, Appollo presided over Delphi for nine months, then, during the winter, it was Dionysus's principal shrine). Previously, irrationality had traditionally been associated with the feminine. The ancients revered prophecy, intuition, and altered states of consciousness. That the god of irrationality, Dionysus, was now a man cloaked in feminine garb is but another awkward artifice enabling a male god to usurp feminine attributes."

Most Greek gods were thought to be invisible—not Dionysus. The boy-god was one of the few the Greeks represented in a frontal depiction; his red face and red body makeup has "enlivened cavorting maskers in celebrations up through the Renaissance, and lives on today in masked revelers of Mardi Gras and Halloween....Virtually all the Dionysian characteristics," Shlain continues, "mentioned: figs, bulls, Muses, the moon, dance, music, moisture, serpents, sexuality, regeneration of the earth, the cultivation of plants, and the nonverbal expressiveness of the mask, were originally under the aegis of the Goddess."

As a result of these events, depression and suicide became prevalent for Greek women. In the city-state of Miletus, the king found it necessary to post a proclamation "that any woman who died by her own hand would have her naked corpse carried through the streets.

"It was the women more than the men who actually experienced the pain, terror, and death of the god's dark side in Dionysian rituals. At the Agrionia festival in Orchomenus, a trumpet blast signaled a group of young girls to begin running, literally for their lives. A Dionysian priest chased after them brandishing a sword. Any girl he overtook, he struck dead. In Arcadian Alea, the festivities began with the flogging of women."

Beginning in the eighth century B.C.—simultaneous with the public embrace of the written word—women were relegated to the margins of Greek culture. Nowhere is this better illustrated than in the vast differences between the cities of Sparta and Athens.

Spartan society was based around the military; they held literacy in extremely low esteem; mental discipline more suited their philosophy of life. According to historian Edith Hamiliton, "The Spartans have left the world nothing in the way of art, literature, or science. Lycurgus, who formulated their law, did not commit it to writing. He ordered everyone to memorize it. Plutarch writes that there was even a Spartan law against committing any law to writing. The Spartan code of conduct glorified deprivation and cruelty; their government was oligarchic with fascist leanings."

Athens, on the other hand, is thought to have assembled some of history's greatest creative thinkers. Lucky for us, these men reduced their ideas to writing. The people of Athens assigned great importance to drama, literature, and philosophy. They were the first to give democracy an extended opportunity to flourish. But women were also considered second-class members of society. Athenians regularly banned women from education, government, and public affairs. "Solon, the Athenian lawgiver, denied women the right to buy or sell land. As in the Old Testament, his code placed women under the men's guardianship. An Athenian father retained the right to dissolve his daughter's marriage."

Such was not the case in Sparta. At every level of that society, women were revered or co-equal with men. Women's clothes, their education, even their sports competition were done in equality with males. Motherhood and warrior-hood were considered noble callings and of equal value to the entire culture. "Spartan women ruled in the absence of their men…By the fourth century B.C., women owned two-fifths of all Spartan land."

Athens and Sparta afford us an opportunity to examine the validity of the theory of what happened to a culture once they embraced writing. On the surface Athens and Sparta seemed so much alike. "Both were Greek. Both worshipped the same deities. They spoke and wrote a common language. They were contemporaneous. Both were bellicose. And yet the difference distinguishing the two city-states was their attitudes toward the alphabet."

Against this background, it's clear that in the Middle East, Southern Europe, and most of the *western* world during the first millennium B.C., the Goddess had virtually disappeared. However, there was another half of the world we haven't mentioned.

d5. The Eastern World:

For purposes of reference, humankind decided long ago to refer to the two hemispheres of this planet we call earth as East and West. The West is generally thought to include Western Europe, North and South America, and Australia. The rest of Europe, Asia, and Africa, comprise the East. No overview of the disappearance of the Goddess would be complete without a brief historical inspection of events taking place in the East during the three millennia before the birth of Christ.

India

India is also a part of the East; modern Indian culture traces its beginnings back to Mohenjo-Daro. "Situated on the rich alluvial plain of the Indus River high in the northwest corner of India, this ancient urban complex, excavated in the 1920s, stands as mute testimony to a highly advanced culture that flourished from 2500 B.C. to 1500 B.C. Composed of sturdy brick buildings laid out along handsome wide avenues, the city was more than three miles in circumference and was home to more than thirty-five thousand inhabitants. This ancient culture is called Harappan; named after Harappa, Mohenjo-Daro's twin city.

"Although they flowered about five hundred years later than either Egypt or Mesopotamia, the Indus Valley cities rank as one of the progenitor civilizations of modern society. The citizenry was well versed in craft and metallurgy. The Harappans built a complex network of irrigation channels to carry the waters of the Indus River to distant fields. Their sailors made trade voyages to Sumer and Egypt as early as 3000 B.C.

"The large majority of artifacts resembling humans appear to be statues of a Mother Goddess. From the archaeological record and present anthropological studies of customs in remoter areas of the subcontinent, a picture has emerged suggesting that all across India there once flourished relatively egalitarian, Goddess-worshipping cultures."

These people spoke an early form of *sanskrit* and created an early form of writing which contained over 500 pictographic characters. Historians believe this Harappan culture composed epic poems known as Vedas which addressed complicated issues concerning religion and philosophy. The reason no one knows for certain about the origin of these poems is that they were not reduced to writing in the early *sanskrit* language, thereby suggesting its difficulty of use.

However, when Aryan warriors invaded from the north in about 1500 B.C., they already knew something of the alphabet. Historians know this from diplomatic letters they discovered from the Aryan Hittites who wrote them from what is now Persia and Turkey dating back to 1450 B.C. The result was that theses invaders adapted their Semitic language to the *sanskrit* and eventually produced the Brahami script (The Aryans developed the Aramaic alphabet, an offshoot of the Semitic). It took another thousand years before it was ready to express literature—the Vedas.

"The Aryans grafted onto these ancient poems their own version of cosmic events, as victorious cultures often do, superimposing their values on the Harappans. A careful reading of the Vedas, however, suggests the takeover of a barely literate, agricultural, but highly sophisticated, egalitarian society by a militaristic, patriarchal alphabetic one....The Rig-Veda is India's oldest epic poem and contains glimpses of the culture as it existed before the arrival of the Aryan warriors and alphabet literacy. Women held considerable power and possessed the all-important right to own property. They participated freely at feasts and rituals. Widows could remarry. Darpaudi, a heroine in the Mahabharata, was married to five brothers simultaneously. Although a latter text than the Rig-Veda, the fact remains that polyandry is mentioned at all suggests that in the transitional Indian Epic Age (2000-1000 B.C.) women enjoyed many prerogatives. (Polyandry continued in

Ceylon [Sri Lanka] until 1859, and still exists in remoter villages of the Himalayan foothills and in Tibet.)"

The philosophical section of the Vedas was called the Upanishad and was written by well-known authors, among the wisest of which were a man, Yajinavalkya, and a woman, Gargi. The fact that a woman enjoyed such an exalted position indicates a non-patriarchal society—one where a gentle creation story filled with pre-Aryan characteristics could exist and thrive. "It attributes the world to a single, irrepressible Pro-creator. This original Being was a fusion of male and female and, in form, resembled 'a woman and a man closely embraced.' Desiring companionship, it split itself into two pieces.

> ...therefrom arose a husband (*pati*) and a wife (*patri*). Therefore...one's self is like a half fragment;...therefore this space is filled by a wife. He copulated with her. Therefore humans beings were produced. And she bethought herself: "How, now, does he copulate with me after we have from each other come? Come let me hide myself." She became a cow. He became a bull. With her he did indeed copulate. Then cattle were born. She became a mare, he a stallion...The horses were born.

"The female and the male continue this charming dance, populating the world with all living things. The original being then proudly proclaims, 'I, indeed, am this creation, for I emitted it all from myself.'"

From these Vedas it is easy to see that in the Indian culture all living things are god—the universe is god. "The Hindu formula for spirituality is 'I *am* Thou.'" You and I and the rest of creation are a part of the world of His *image*. It is the only world.

In contrast, western cultures recognize a monotheistic God who is at once in all of us and the rest of the universe, but also extends beyond that to all the universes of all the universes and beyond that to infinity and then beyond that. He is without end or limitation. He simply is.

The Aryans warriors completed their conquest of India by 1250 B.C. and "settled down to a life of tillage and herding." Nevertheless, the differences between East and West were stark indeed. "In contrast to the Israelites and the Greeks, Aryan priests [Brahmins], recognizing the power inherent in alphabet words, tightly controlled who could learn to read and write. The Old Testament commanded ordinary Israelites to read scripture, and every male Greek was expected to have read the *Iliad*." If a member of the working class was "convicted of reciting the Vedas, he would have his tongue split; if he possessed a written text, he would be cut in two."

As time passed, the Brahmins began to assume more and more positions of leadership previously held by women; slowly the liberties enjoyed by women began to disappear. The Hindu civilization maintained itself for 2000 years without any written code of law. It wasn't until around 300 B.C. that the priestly class presented "an alphabetic civil code" called the Laws of Manu. They now contained many denigrating passages concerning women: "The source of all dishonor is woman; the source of strife is woman; therefore avoid women."

Yet to this day, India still worships its gods and goddesses. "Despite the Aryans', Greeks', and Muslim' attempts to impose masculine left-brain values on Indian culture, they were only partially successful....Hindus venerate the *lingam* and *yoni*, sculptural forms that represent, respectively, the equality of the male and female generative forces"

In 533 B.C., Buddhism sprung to life in India; founded by Siddharta Gautama, a married Indian noble, it eventually became another patriarchal religion based on an alphabetic sacred text. In the beginning it attracted wide-spread interest throughout all segments of Indian society. During the centuries that followed, it grew rapidly and then suddenly went into decline, another victim of India's fiercely anti-patriarchal mentality. By 500 A.D., Buddhism was virtually extinct in India. Today, less than one percent of the Indian population call themselves Buddhists. However, throughout the rest of the East, Buddhism grew like wildfire, especially in India's large neighbor to the north—China.

China & the Rest of the East

Despite the best efforts of the patriarchal leaders who came later, the archeological and cultural evidence suggests that pre-literate China also enjoyed considerable egalitarian and right-brained attitudes toward women. Chinese folklore refers to a time when "'people knew their mothers but not their fathers,' a cryptic allusion to an age of matrilineal succession. (Even in present-day China, there remains enclaves that retain matrilineal inheritance customs; for example, the Nashi culture.)...Ancient Chinese family names were built up from the symbol representing 'woman.'...An ancient written Chinese characters for 'wife' also meant 'equal.'...The character for 'roof' over the character for 'woman' denotes 'peace.'...In ancient times, a wife kept her own name after marriage."

In 1500 B.C. while much of the Western world was embracing the alphabet, the oldest Chinese characters first appeared—carved into tortoise shells and bones. They "transformed mental ideas into concrete *images*. Their use of a pictographic written language instead of an alphabetic one strongly affected their historical development. Along with ancient Hebrew, Chinese is the oldest continuously used written language.

"Writing of any kind will realign the gender politics of any culture. A main factor promoting ancient China's patriarchy was...the change in cultural perception that accompanies the acquisition of the art of writing. Although the writing happened to be more right-brained than the style developed in the West, and produced subtle changes unique to China, the country still experienced a shift in which men appropriated power."

Literacy in this huge country began to take root with the general population around six hundred B.C. It was then that two major and entirely different philosophies appeared: Taoism and Confucianism. "Their respective founders, Lao-tzu and Confucius, were contemporaries. Taoism represented an egalitarian feminine viewpoint from the past. Confucianism championed masculine dominance and became the creed of the future.

"Taoism promoted Mother *nature* as the guiding force, while Confucianism touted Father *culture*. At their founding, Taoism and Confucianism both lacked a deity. Both were humanistic, practical guides to living. Both had strong opinions about women, writing, and images.

"Lao-tzu transformed the mystery of the feminine spirit into his enigmatic rendering of the Tao using primarily the metaphor of horizontally flowing water. 'The great Tao flows everywhere, both to the left and to the right...it holds nothing back. It fulfills its purpose silently and makes no claims.' In contrast, Confucius' system rested on a hierarchical ordering of the world. Its foundation was the family. But Confucius' idea of family values depended on a wife's obedience. The Confucian/yang need to control stands in stark contrast to the Tao/yin admonition that the sage should never try to control anything. In Taoism, intuition was the guide to wisdom. Reason and reading the classics were the basic of Confucianism."

Around 200 B.C., a government official "standardized Chinese ideographs," which then made writing much easier for everyday use. Simultaneously, interest in Confucianism rose, and "women's rights in China began a decline from which they have not recovered." Sometime during the first century B.C., the emperor Wu Ti declared Confucianism "the official religion of the state and this text became the basis for all subsequent Confucian doctrine." Thereafter, biographies of women virtually vanished.

Initially, Confucianism enjoyed a growth spurt, but soon this dynasty ended and China entered its "Dark Ages." This was when Confucianism fell into decline and "the essential feminine nature of Chinese culture reasserted itself. Taoists gradually superseded the Confucians. Another factor in the decline of Confucianism was the defection of followers to Buddhism, which had arrived from India in the first century A.D. Despite the rapid growth of Buddhism in China, Taoism remained the dominant philosophical force in the early centuries of the Common Era."

But then again, by the first millennium A.D., Confucianism enjoyed an amazing resurgence and soared past Taoism, but with it came a return to the mistreatment of women. "The most misogynist practice, epitomizing Confucian attitudes toward women, was the custom of foot-binding. Linen strips tightly wound around a young girl's growing feet deformed the bones in such a manner that the top of the forefoot bent back and under itself. A woman had to learn to walk, if she could, on what should have been the uppermost surfaces of her toes. Many adult upper class women were unable to walk and had to be carried by servants, but only with a mincing gait. This practice began because Chinese men found this deformity sexually stimulating."

Around this same time, several other events took place in China worth noting: The printing press began to dominate Chinese society; patriarchy once again superseded egalitarianism; lawmakers formulated their first effective universal code of written laws; and the idea of imageless monotheism gained national acceptance. Anything female was thought to be weak, ineffectual, and a necessary evil that the male-driven society had to overcome. Once again, MTS was in power; WTS and goddesses were "out."

Priests were forbidden to marry or indulge in any sexual contact. Human images—especially female images which depicted their sexuality—were strongly discouraged from all public artwork. Buddha now became a kind of ubiquitous middle-aged female —almost doleful and hermaphroditic in appearance—so as to co-op potential public assertions of misogynism. The Goddess had to be robbed of her beauty and sexuality. This practice soon spread throughout the rest of the East.

"Compare most statues of the Buddha from Japan to Korea with his depictions in nearby Southeast Asia, Indonesia, the Philippines, or Tibet; the differences are striking. The lands that honored the feminine and had poorly developed literary traditions retain the Buddha's masculine form. The most earnest efforts to the literate Japanese, Korean, and Chinese patriarchs could not suppress the spirit or the image of the Great Goddess, even if they disguised her as a man."

As mentioned earlier, in Northern Africa—especially Egypt—the role of the Great Goddess had paralleled, in general terms, that which was taking place in the rest of the Middle East. The Egyptians, like many of their neighbors, had invented their own alphabet, and soon their female deities began to fade from their once preeminent positions. Slowly the writing itself took on another appearance—a more horizontal script. With these changes came a cultural lurch toward patriarchy. Shlain writes: "In every society that learned the written word, the female deity lost ground to the male deity. Before the invention of writing, these two powerful forces had remained entwined in sexual union. In every Mediterranean society that embraced literacy, women lost their hold and fell from grace—economically, politically, and spiritually....The most dramatic changes for women were yet to come; the coming storm was brewing in the lands between Mesopotamia and Egypt."

d6. Timeout in the Middle of The Vanishing Goddess

Because this section forms the backbone of this book, I thought it would help the reader if we were to take a brief timeout and review where we are.

In the fifth or sixth centuries B.C., writing became commonplace in the Western and Eastern hemispheres of the world. In the West, it was the alphabet; in the East it was ideograms. These developments paralleled the demise of the Mother Goddess, the simultaneous mistreatment of women, and the introduction of new spiritual leaders who would later rise to a higher level of consciousness.

Shlain wonders, "Why did misogyny so often accompany their message? The answer: *There is something inherently anti-female in the written word. Men obsessed with the written word tend to be sexist.* The vast majority of men who love women and have families are not the ones who withdraw from conventional life to preach doctrines that others, similarly disposed, commit to writing.... [T]hey [those males who withdrew from life] muddied the waters, as far as women were concerned, so thoroughly that it would take twenty-five hundred years before some women, and a few men, would begin to see through the muddle again."

We'll discuss much more about this in subsequent chapters, but for now we need to focus our attention back to the Middle East and Southern Europe—especially Italy. Another turning point in the course of human events was about to unfold. It all began rather hopefully from a female perspective and that of the goddess.

First, the Greeks departed center stage in 338 B.C. at the hands of the Macedonians, who were, for the most part, illiterate farmers. These conquerors quickly overturned the Athenian idea of democracy and re-instituted the notion of kingship. This meant that women fared far better; now they could again own and manage their own wealth and property. They were now free to mingle with men and hold professional positions throughout all Macedonian society. By 100 B.C., under the rule of Alexander the Great, women held almost equal social status with men, but alas, the world was about to undergo a monolith the likes of which had not been seen before.

d7. The Romans:

By 49 B.C., Julius Caesar had defied the Roman Senate and with his army crossed the Rubicon into Rome; he had already "handily defeated the rump remains of Alexander's empire." After his assassination, the Roman Empire would last another five hundred years and, at its height, encompass "more than 1,250,000 square miles with a total population of over 60,000,000 people [well over 50% of the estimated then-world's total population including Northern Africa]." So in the size and duration of their Empire, the Romans were much more successful than the Greeks, but in new ideas and intellectual innovation, they relied heavily on copying the best of the past and calling it their own.

One such variation on this well-established conqueror's trick was their approach to religion. "The Romans exhibited their lack of imagination by imitating Greek myth and ritual. By the fourth century B.C., they had transferred their allegiances to all the gods of Greece's Mount Olympus, changing only the deities' names. Perhaps because they had blithely co-opted another people's mythology in their early centuries, Roman authorities, to their credit, were extremely tolerant of others' beliefs.

"Whereas the Greeks had maintained a strict separation between religious and secular realms, the Romans made religion an integral part of the State. This policy helped them pacify and assimilate newly conquered people by offering them citizenship. Because of the legal, mercantile, and educational opportunities accompanying such a passport , the offer became a coveted honor for people annexed into the Empire. The vanquished had only to acknowledge the Roman gods and the divinely inspired *genius* of the emperor. Officials distributed images of the current ruler throughout the empire. Subjects seeking dispensations paid obeisance to the Roman man-god by publicly bowing before his likeness. The Romans did not ask that anyone forswear his own religion. These reasonable terms made the offer difficult to refuse among the polyglot of peoples comprising the Empire. The only ones who objected to these conditions were the Jews. Acknowledging the great antiquity of the 'People of the Book,' the Romans made an exception for them so the Jews could maintain fealty to their solitary deity. And out of respect for the Jewish proscriptions against images, Roman governors assigned to Judea ordered their troops traveling through Judean crowds to cover up the flags emblazoned with the effigy of the emperor." The Jewish male god had been well-established and no goddesses were to be allowed there.

But in Roman society, the Greek Dionysus became the Roman Bacchus; the spiritual side of Dionysus became the Roman Orpheus. Soon Romans of all classes and backgrounds embraced the Orphic cult, and tried to pursue lives "above reproach." Roman gods stood at the center of all Roman culture, but many sensed they weren't enough. "The heightened sense of spirituality associated with Orphanism primed the populace for a new religion. Another new god was coming. In 40 B.C., the poet Virgil wrote, 'Now...the great line of centuries begins anew...Only do thou, sweet Lucina, smile on the birth of a child, under whom the iron brood shall first cease, and a golden race spring up throughout the world!'"

Under the Romans, women gradually regained some of the ground they had lost in most of the Greek societies. "Roman women basked in the prerogatives granted them by a regime enthralled by the images of its art. But the plethora of statues tended to obscure a dearth of gritty thinkers....A spiritual vacuum was hollowing out the center of the Roman Empire even as the battle standards of its legions continued to sweep outwards. This vortex would generate a new religion as all the expectant longings of the disparate classes swirling around in the first century coalesced. No one then alive could have anticipated that a tornado cloud was forming over Judea. The funnel would touch down in a place called Golgotha, and when the debris settled four centuries later, the landscape would be permanently changed. An entirely new paradigm of reality would replace the classical one; images would become objects of revulsion among the adherents of a new religion, who would turn on them on a scale unprecedented in history. Statues, unable to run for their lives, were toppled, their noses, ears, and limbs disfigured with such thoroughness that few escaped this artistic holocaust. And women in the new religion would lose the short-lived, hard-won gains they had wrested from the Roman Imperial Empire."

d8. The Early Christians

It's essential to remember the reason we're spending so much time following the plight of women through the course of history: powerful Goddesses existed only in cultures where women were held in high regard. The historic fact is that when women and men worked together as equals, that spirit of cooperation usually followed as a natural result of the religious beliefs of that culture—where Goddesses were the most meaningful religious icon. It should be clear to the reader by this point that when male gods have played a dominant role in a culture, the predictable outcome has virtually always been a corresponding mistreatment of women by the males.

Jesus as a religious icon is not the Jesus I wish to address. I want to discuss the historical Jesus. What makes Him so interesting and unusual in terms of this book is that He was a male god born from the womb of a real woman. Furthermore, although much of what He is alleged to have said was embraced by the early followers of Christianity, on the subject of women these so-called people of God chose to ignore what Jesus modeled. So we have to differentiate between what He stood for and any religion that claims His teachings as their foundation.

Although I personally have mixed feelings about religion and the role it plays in modern society, the fact remains that a Jewish man called Jesus of Nazareth lived. He was a prophet and, according to eye-witnesses, performed more than a few so-called miracles. Furthermore, he preached a new philosophy of life—one that astounded, confounded, and inspired those who heard him. But in order to better understand how bewildering His words must have been to these Israelites, we first of all need to go back and immerse ourselves into the thinking of the Jewish people in last century B.C..

For more than 600 years a passage written in Second Isaiah had raised the issue of a savior: "For unto us a child is born, a son is given; and the government shall be upon his shoulders, and his name shall be called...the mighty God, the Prince of Peace (Isa.9:6)." Other books of the Old Testament talked about a "Son of God," a savior, and a *Messiah*, but those were the days of the warrior. All men of great standing were kings or mighty generals; all power came from the point of a sword, shield, and the number of men one could deliver into battle at any given moment. The Jews prayed and anticipated that Yahweh's representative would, in one fell swoop, rectify all social inequities.

"In the years closing out the B.C. era, this idea steadily gained force. The Essenes, a very religious Jewish sect, abandoned society to live in isolated desert communities to prepare for the coming confrontation. They recreated the austere conditions Israelites experienced during their wandering. Essenes lived a pious communal life. They believed that the Messiah would be an earthly military commander who would lead them to victory in the war against the sinful, and they trained to be Yahweh's soldiers in the battle of Armageddon, the ultimate conflict between the forces of good and evil.

"The god of Moses and Abraham had been nowhere and everywhere, but in the Herodian era He [the Jewish god] was presumed by many to dwell in the Temple's inner sanctum. [In 43 B.C. Rome appointed Herod to oversee fiercely independent and rebellious Judea. Their

Temple had been destroyed by Nebuchadnezzar in 597 B.C. and the Jews had long prayed for its reconstruction. As a way to curry favor with the Jews, Harod rebuilt and enlarged the Temple so that it now became one of the architectural wonders of the entire Roman Empire. It sat on a 35-acre complex and the outside perimeter walls of the Temple itself measured over a mile.] This belief enabled the [Jewish] priesthood to wield absolute authority over religious matters. The Sadduces, the Temple's clerical upper class, dominated the Sanhedrin, the Council of Elders, and were intent on maintaining the *status quo*. By building this immense edifice, Herod, the non-Jew, had unwittingly changed the character of Judaism." [The practice of animal sacrifice in the re-built Temple had now taken on an assembly-line efficiency. One pilgrim from Alexandria wrote home that he had "witnessed seven hundred priests each performing multiple sacrifices during a single day." The smells from blood-drenched floors and burnt offerings together with the blasts of horns and the lowing of terrified animals must have traumatized the senses of all visitors.]

Politically, unrest festered in all the Roman provinces. According to Shlain, "The disparity between the sybaritic lifestyle of the wealthy few and the misery of the numerous downtrodden had dangerously unbalanced society. Rebellion was in the air. In 4 B.C., the Romans crucified two thousand Jews in Galilee for sedition and left their rotting corpses on a forest of crosses as a warning to others.

"Increasingly, Jews began to question the direction their ancient faith was heading. Pharisees—mostly middle-class lawyers and merchants— were more liberal than the fundamentalist Sadduces and believed that reform lay in reinterpreting the Torah with new wisdom writings such as the Talmud. They expended considerable intellectual energy interpreting Mosiac law to make it more congruent with the realities of the times. Un- fortunately, many of their legalistic explanations seemed to some like splitting hairs."

In retrospect, it's easy to see why no one paid much attention when a "charismatic faith healer named Jesus of Nazareth began preaching to the communities around the shores of Galilee." This area was known for its revolutionary attitudes so when He spoke for the disenfranchised, people listened, but never saw Him as a threat to the mighty Romans. His message was all about nurturement, not war or battle. He spoke out against classism, the reductionism of the Pharisees, the fundamentalism of the Sadduces, and the zealotry of the Essenes. He spoke of love—a selfless love—of one's neighbor. He spoke against the traditionally patriarchal attitudes of Jewish life. He spoke of forgiveness of one's enemies; in "Jesus' eyes, the poor, the disabled, and women were equal to the richest slave owner." He was a trouble-maker and had to be eliminated.

"Women were drawn to Jesus' ministry. He treated then with kindness and respect, even if they were infirm, prostitutes, or adulteresses. His message resonated within the hearts of women, who had been consigned to marginal roles in the prevailing patriarchal religions....Since divorce favored husbands, Jesus' inflexible position protected married women. Old women, fearful that their husbands would trump up an excuse to abandon them for a younger wife, found comfort and security in Jesus' teaching on the matter.

"In his majestic Sermon on the Mount, Jesus taught that every person has the capacity and responsibility to distinguish between good and evil. Love, compassion, free will, and nonviolence combined with a disregard for laws, money, and power expressed a feminine agenda such as no Western religious leader had ever before espoused."

But Jesus asked His followers to memorize His message and not preserve it in any written format. He consistently criticized those who relied on the written word to understand and live their faith. ("Our qualification comes from God, who has indeed qualified us ministers of a new covenant, not of letter but of spirit, for the letter brings death and the spirit brings life."—2 Corinthians 3: 3-6) Yet after His death, it was

Paul who returned to his own pre-disposition in favor of Pharisee-like thinking (that of heavy reliance upon the written word). "It is paradoxical that men like Paul who wrote at length about Love with a big L seem to have been incapable of loving any one particular woman, a relationship far more demanding of commitment than sitting alone in a room writing about Love in the abstract. Women's influence in the new movement, however, concerned him, and he tried to restrict their power.

"Former slaves, rogues, criminals, and peoples of every ethnicity receiving Christ became qualified to teach and have authority over congregations. Only women were excluded from this privilege. This exception brought Paul's doctrine into conflict with Jesus' principal teaching concerning equality. Paul justified his position by assailing Eve for her sin.

"In the first decades after Jesus' death, women played a prominent role in the church, and in several of his epistles Paul pays tribute to them. But despite his *pro forma* chivalry, Paul's edicts concerning a woman's place in the church soon became dogma, and it became impossible for a woman to conduct so much as a minor religious ceremony in the new religion."

So much for following the word of their so-called Savior.

It had now been more than 3000 years since Mother Goddess held a prominent position in society. Yet with the story of Jesus, his mother, and her husband (Joseph), the possibility of a new Mother Goddess had once again become a reality. But the early Christians weren't having any of that; Paul and his followers made sure to scuttle that idea. Within a 100 years of His death, the early Christians began writing down the story of Jesus, His life, and teachings. As this process gained momentum, the role of women receded.

It didn't happen all at once. First, there was the confrontations between the Orthodox and the Gnostics. "To the Orthodox, the *written* scriptures were divine revelation. In the Gnostic tradition, spiritual instructions were given and received *orally*. The ultimate achievement of Gnosis was to have an insight of such crystalline clarity that one became a Christ. The Orthodox condemned this idea as arrogant. The Gnostics derided the Orthodox claim that baptism was the first station on an arduous road to Truth.

"The battle between the Gnostic and Orthodox wings of Christianity began within a generation after the Crucifixion and raged for several centuries. Both sides were evenly matched in terms of talented leaders and persuasive proselytizers. But in A.D. 313, when the Roman conqueror Constantine declared that Christianity was the state religion, he chose the Orthodox to administer it.

"The victory of the Orthodox over the Gnostics marked a turning point for Western civilization. Although much of the quarrel between the two factions was couched in abstruse arguments, the Orthodox/Gnostic struggle was at its core a conflict between words and images. One translation of the Greek *ortho-doxy* could be 'straight thinking' or in the context of this book, 'linear thinking.' *Gnosis* is the Greek word for knowledge. The Greeks distinguished between *epistene*, knowledge acquired from facts, and *gnosis*, which we call 'intuition.' In the first schism of the nascent church, the Orthodox and the Gnostics split along the lines of the hemispheres of the brain. The linear thinkers favored left-brain, male-dominated patriarchies, heavy on guilt, dogma, obedience, and the literature of the Christ story. The intuiters were more often egalitarian and were entranced by the mythopoesis of Jesus' life and death."

But with his decision to embrace the Orthodox, Constantine forever changed the world. Patriarchy and misogynism had once again followed the written word. Christianity had missed its chance. The concept of Goddess, at least for another thousand years, was dead. The reader is strongly invited to mark well this historical moment. It will play a momentous role in the reversal of fortunes for the concept of goddess.

d9. The Dark Ages—A Brief Reversal

With the defeat of the last Roman emperor in 476 A.D. at the hands of the German chieftain Odoacer, the Middle or Dark Ages of our planet earth began. War became a way of life for most of the world. The high literacy rate of the Romans quickly fell into serious neglect and use of the alphabet became almost nonexistent except for the nobility. The only institution which maintained its use was the Church—the Catholic Church, which by now had been, thanks to Constantine, established as the only church throughout all of the Roman Empire. Kenneth Clark speculates that "for five hundred years, no king or nobleman could read. While there were occasional exceptions in lay society, a lampblack illiteracy descended over most of Europe, unbalancing culture.

"The Dark Ages was a black hole out from which not a single significant scientific, literary, or philosophical idea emerged. Without a written record, historians have had to piece together a sense of what life was like in the Dark Ages largely by inference and deduction. The diorama they have assembled is most unsettling. Barbarous practices, ignorance, and superstition apparently ruled. In the words of Thomas Hobbes, life was 'nasty, brutish, and short.'"

At or near the beginning of the second millennium (1000), literacy began to make a comeback, but strangely enough so did feminist values. "Poets, bards, jongleurs, and troubadors were singing the praises of womanhood. From out of the pitch-black womb of the Dark Ages emerged the Age of Chivalry, in which the highest aspiration of a man was to protect and serve 'the fair sex.'" Equality of and cooperation between the sexes reached heights not seen in more than 1500 years. According to historian Doris Stenton, "The evidence which has survived…indicates that women were more nearly companions of their husbands and brothers than at any other period before the modern age."

Perhaps the goddess as a cultural necessity was about to make a comeback.

d10. A French Possibility

Enter King Arthur and the Knights of the Round Table to the world stage. Told by traveling minstrels and inspired by the Chivalric Age, it wasn't until the 15th century that author Thomas Mallory assembled the highlights of Arthur's reign into one cohesive story. There's still considerable debate among historians whether or not any part of it was reality. "Above all, this oral culture taught men how to be *courteous.* Arthur's most trusted advisor was the wizard Merlin. Wizards are shamans and they were held in high regard during the time of orality."

In 1337, the Hundred Years War broke out in France. The basis of the war was an attempt by the English crown to annex France by force of arms. That war finally ended in 1453 when Charles VII of France defeated the last stubborn English troops (The War of Roses was also just beginning back in England). According to legend, Merlin had predicted the turning point in the Hundred Years' War as early as 800 A.D. when he wrote that France would be "betrayed by a woman and saved by a virgin." The time was right for the appearance of a goddess-warrior on the world stage.

Jeanne d'Arc (known as Joan of Arc to most Americans) was born in 1412 on a small farm on the border of northeastern France. It was a time of magic, superstition, fear, and deeply held faith; Catholicism was still the religion of all Europe. Like most girls her age, Joan could neither read nor write (the only people who could read and write in those days were the clergy and some of the noblemen and royalty). Not only that, Joan hated war and battle. She'd seen too many of her beloved neighbors and friends victimized or killed by marauding troops from the raging war. Several times, the girl, her family, and close friends had been forced to leave their farms and take refuge in neighboring villages while the war careened out of control across the rolling Lorraine district countryside.

In 1420 when Jeanne was eight, Queen Isabella of France, mother of Charles VII—the then 17-year-old crown prince (his official title was the *Dauphin*)—signed a treaty with England and the French House of Burgundy which basically denied Charles the right to succeed to the throne. The Treaty of Troyes (its official name) provided for the King of England to assume the role of King of France once the boy's insane father, Charles VI, had died. The first half of the Merlin prophecy had been fulfilled.

When she was twelve, Joan began experiencing inexplicable visits from what she believed were messengers from God (she later identified them in her trial as Saint Catherine, Saint Margaret, and Saint Michael the Archangel). She kept these visitors a secret from all the world and referred to them as her Voices because they often communicated to her without actually speaking. At first, they only asked her to work on her faith and develop a closer relationship with God. Since she was already an extremely pious girl for her age and time, that wasn't all that difficult a request. She willingly complied and a few years later, the girl pledged her life to the service of God and, unknown to her parents and siblings, made a personal vow to her Voices of virginity in the service of God.

When Joan was 16, her Voices began telling her it was time for her to fulfill God's plan for her life. She needed to leave her parents' farm, they stated, and go help the *Dauphin* become King of all France. They also told her that she only had about a year to complete God's work. Confused but willing, she finally convinced Robert Baudricourt, governor and royal lieutenant of the region—Vaucouleurs—to arrange an audience for her with Charles VII. It was March 1429.

By July of that same year and after many brutal battles, the illiterate farm girl had crowned the *Dauphin* King of France (the Battle of

Orleans is generally considered the turning point of the Hundred Years' War). In May of 1430, she was accidentally captured by the Burgundians; at first they didn't even know it was she. On May 30, 1431, the Catholic Church and the English burned her at the stake in Rouen as a witch and a heretic.

After that, things move rather slowly in terms of Joan's goddess stature: 1453: the 100 Years' War ends. 1456: Rehabilitation hearings about the validity of Joan's trial end—she is found innocent of witchcraft and heresy; Joan's sentence of 1431 is annulled; she and her family name cleared (Charles had ennobled her whole family in December of 1429 as a gesture of thanks for her contribution to the military victories of that year as well as her role in having him crowned King.) Charles VII dies July 22, 1461; his reign is considered one of the most important in the history of France because of his ability to reunite the nation and heal the emotional wounds brought by the War.

For the next four centuries, the question of what to do about Joan of Arc becomes captive to a deadly power struggle between French politicians and the Catholic Church. Finally, the University of Paris admits their grievous role in this national tragedy and the dam breaks. 1869: Jeanne is proposed as a saint to Pope Pious IX; January 24,1894: Pope Leo XIII declares there's just cause to seek her beatification. January 6, 1904: Pope Pious X issues a decree of *heroic virtue*. April 18, 1909: beatification takes place at St. Peter's Basilica. May 16, 1920: Pope Benedict XV canonizes Joan; May 30th becomes her liturgical feast day; May 8th (second Sunday in May; the day the Joan kicked the English out of Orleans) is a national holiday in all France for Joan—voted June 24, 1920 by the French parliament.

In 1894, Louis Kossuth—a world renowned Hungarian author, freedom fighter, and politician—would write about this incredible young woman: "Consider this unique and imposing distinction. Since the writing of human history began, Joan of Arc is the ONLY (emphasis added) person, of either sex, who has ever held supreme command of the military forces of a nation *at the age of seventeen.*"

Before 1429, Joan of Arc had never ridden a horse, held a sword, or participated in any battle or military episode of any kind. Contrary to what recent movies and novels may depict, she was not attractive—short, ordinary of face, and muscular from working in the fields and around the farm. During her entire 19 years, she never learned to read or write. She did learn to dictate letters which she often sent prior to battles against the English and Burgundians. She would send them a note requesting their surrender so as to give the generals an opportunity to save their men's lives. In the beginning, the experienced military men always laughed, then Joan and her French troops would rout them. Soon, opposing forces would begin their retreat once they saw Joan ride into battle, her white flag of God flapping in the breeze.

She never personally killed anyone. She never understood military strategy—only what her Voices insisted had to be accomplished. When opposing armies had been defeated, she always gave them a chance to retreat without further military encounter. It drove her generals and soldiers to distraction, but never did her anti-militaristic philosophy work to the detriment of her cause. On days of battle, she seldom ate anything other than bread, wine, and water—if that. She dressed like a man from the moment she left Vaucouleurs, but never swore. She attended mass every day and insisted that her soldiers do the same—much to the great surprise of her cynical generals, the soldiers agreed. She also demanded that her troops not swear and that prostitutes no longer be allowed into camp; the men readily agreed. They too knew of the Merlin prediction and believed it to the very marrow of their being. And after a few initial winning skirmishes just prior to the Battle of Orleans, any remaining doubts were immediately quashed. The men of Joan's army wanted to be in her service; many rode from great distances to be in her service. Many had previously quit the service of Charles VII out of frustration, lack of pay, or the severity of their wounds. Joan's unremitting call for the reunification of all France against the hated English and their traitorous allies, the House of Burgundy, was Joan's clarion cry. The common people of France loved her.

Her life and heroic in-battle exploits (especially her physical courage in the heat of battle as well as in her many attempts to escape jail—once she jumped 60 feet at night from the roof of a building onto the stone paving of a street and would have escaped had the force of her landing not knocked her unconscious; when her captors found her, they thought she was dead) were well-chronicled because of the many official inquiries into her life both during her life and after. To this day, the record of her various trials are carefully preserved in French government archives for all who seek to verify the accuracy of her story. Much of what occurred in the rest of the world during that same time period has been reconstructed and extrapolated by historians from remaining evidence and skimpy records, but in the case of Joan's life, there's little to surmise. Everything about her life—her childhood friends and neighbors, what kind of a child she was, how she was raised, her piety, her personality, her appearance and clothes, her bad temper, her extraordinary humility, her intelligence, her great verbal skills, her love of her fellow human beings and all living creatures, her illiteracy, her inability to ride horseback, her lack of military training of any sort, and on and on—has been checked and double-checked. None of it has been invented.

The emergence of this potential warrior-goddess on the world scene has been a subject of great controversy for nearly six hundred years. Most English-speaking male historical observers tend to minimize her accomplishments, while most female experts tend to hold her in high regard. (A recent book on the 100 most important women in the history of the world by a woman author listed Joan of Arc around number 50.) However, there a few male historians who see her contributions as worthy of great admiration. Several see the Battle of Orleans as one of the most important turning points in the history of the world. Unagruably, she saved France from being annexed by the English; without her presence at the Battle of Orleans, the French most assuredly would have lost the encounter, thus allowing an English take-over of Southern France—they already controlled most of the north. Without France, there would have been no successful American Revolutionary War almost 350 years later, and therefore no United States.

Clearly, Jeanne d'Arc is unique in the history of the world. It's no wonder the French bristle at the ignorance of most Americans concerning their incredible *Maid du Pucelle*. We'll discuss the 21st century status of this warrior-goddess in a subsequent chapter. Suffice to say, few non-religious men have much good to say about her today, despite her obvious accomplishments and contributions to the world.

d11. A Jewish Possibility

As mentioned earlier, the Dark Ages were largely characterized by a rejection of the use of the written word and a return to a more barbaric lifestyle. But somewhere around 1000, literacy began to make a comeback in Europe and across the entirety of what had once been the Holy Roman Empire, and, strangely, so did more enlightened societal attitudes toward women. The Age of Chivalry taught MTS that "the highest aspiration of a man was to protect and serve 'the fair sex.'" For the first time in almost two millennia, women and men worked together in a renewed spirit of cooperation and respect. This new standard of conduct had important consequences for Christianity and especially the beginnings of Marianism.

"Mary was an unlikely candidate to become the fourth figure of Christianity after the Trinity. Paul never mentions Jesus' mother, and the Gospel writers make only a few references to her. None acknowledge either her birth or death....Like the Earth Goddess before her, Mary plays a crucial role in only two events in Christ's life: His birth and His death."

The early Church fathers including Paul and Augustine feared a return to polytheism and did all they could to marginalize Earth-mother deities. Basic Christian beliefs were about a divine man, not a divine woman. Nevertheless, "[B]eginning in the Dark Ages, devotion to Mary blossomed throughout European Christendom. The Parthenon of Athena was rededicated to Mary ca. A.D. 600, as were almost all the other extant temples that had honored Pagan goddesses.

"The signal accomplishment of the entire Medieval Age was the erection of great Gothic cathedrals that pierced the skies of Europe with a forest of spires....But the great cathedrals were not dedicated to any of the three male Trinitarian divinities; instead, the four most magnificent cathedrals in France—Paris, Chartres, Reims, and Amiens—are all called *Notre Dame*: Our Lady. So too is Santa Maria del Fior in Florence, Saint Sophia in Constantinople, and the Frauenkirche in Munich. Civic and church leaders dedicated these churches to the *mortal mother* of the Christian deity. In France alone, over a hundred churches and eighty cathedrals were raised in Mary's name....While Mary may not have a gospel extolling her virtues, her rise in stature is eloquently expressed by her highly visible Bible of stone dotting the European landscape....Her subjects came to know her through her *image* that led every procession and adorned the walls of homes, shops, churches, and crossroads. The *likeness* of the Blessed mother became ubiquitous throughout western Europe.

"And a new phenomenon accompanied this change—one that had been absent during Christianity's first four centuries. People reported seeing visions of Mary, though she rarely spoke. Ignorant shepherds and unlettered peasant girls seem to have encountered the spectral Mother far more frequently than learned churchmen. (The [Catholic]

Church has authenticated over twenty-one thousand sightings of Mary.)"

d12. What to do about Mary?

The rise in the popularity of Mary early in the second millennium made the Church fathers uneasy, so they had to do something about the mother of Jesus. "They granted her the honorific "Queen of Heaven," but not "Queen of Earth" or "Queen of the Underworld.""…The male Church hierarchy reverently hailed Mary as Mother of God, but never as God the Mother. To further divorce her from sex and procreation, the Church emphasized two antithetical aspects of Mary: she was the Virgin Mother.

"That the people persisted in honoring Mary as the reincarnation of the ancient Goddess worshipped by all preliterate agrarian civilizations is evidenced by the phenomenon of the Black Virgin. Many medieval churches, extending in a wide arc from Russia across Europe to Spain, had as their most sacred object a statue of a black Mary. The current official papal explanation posits that these representations were blackened by centuries of candle smoke. But close examination reveals that this could not be true, since the statues' clothes are not similarly stained. If soot is not the answer, what is? Why would a Caucasian population, many of whom were blue-eyed and fair-haired, depict the Mother of God as incontrovertibly black?…As with many other aspects of the feminine, the black Mary appeared predominantly in unlettered times and among unlettered populations. Once alphabet literacy regained its hold over human communication, she all but disappeared."

But there was still more work to be done about Mary and her femaleness. Water had long been the symbol of femininity: "In virtually every Creation myth that informs the dawn of civilization, a mother goddess representing the undifferentiated waters created the universe, including Nammu and Tiamat in Sumeria, Vritas and Danu in India, and Tehom and Rehab in several Old Testament psalms. One of Isis's most popular names was Star of the Sea. Mary's name, *Maria*, means water....The Church had to acknowledge Mary's rapidly rising popularity among the common folk. In medieval times the Vatican proclaimed August 15, the Feast of the Assumption, in her honor—by coincidence the same day pagans had honored the goddess Artemis in pre-Christian times. In both France and England, medieval calendars were recalibrated to begin each new year on the Day of Our Lady, March 15."

But, Shlain notes that the Church of the Medieval Ages had to somehow offset her *image* with a new likeness they could invent and control. "In the Old Testament, Yahweh's select few *heard* His voice or *read* His words; in the Medieval Age, people *visualized* her in apparitions....Alphabet cultures know gods through their *words*; non-literate cultures see goddess' *images*...Long ago, when humans were emerging into ego-consciousness," he continues, "Paleolithic peoples painted on rocks and cave walls their universal symbol of the female; archeologists call it 'the vulva sign.' In its most common form, it is an oval with a cleft running up from the bottom. This sign has been identified in cultures of Old Europe, early Mesopotamia, Harappa, and Crete. In an uncanny coincidence, the most evil deity that alphabet religions have ever conjured leaves a mark in the earth that closely resembles the ancient symbol of the Earth Goddess. The devil, although male, conflated symbols previously associated with the Goddess. A foil for Mary was now in place." Shlain proposes that during the medieval period, the Church played on the male fear of women's rising status by piecing together a thinly camouflaged transsexual, diabolical Goddess.

So much for Mary and the Church and a possible return of the Mother Goddess during medieval times, but there are important lessons humankind can draw from these events. Based on what we have seen in history, a strong argument can be made for the interconnectedness of *words* and *images*. Where there is a heavy reliance on the written word—to the virtual exclusion of all else—male gods dominate society, a warrior mentality prevails, and a loss of respect for women follows. Where there is a strong influence in a society of images, a nurturing attitude prevails and female goddesses rise to the level of broad public acceptance—at least for a brief historical moment until MTS figures out how to reassert himself—or so the historical evidence would seem to suggest.

We'll also talk about Mary, the mother of Jesus, and her role in a possible general return to prominence of the Goddess later in the book. The problem is that society and MTS in particular will have to break out of their clichéd patterns of thought. The major question is and will remain: Is *Homo Sapiens* really ready for that?

---

d13. The Reformation

The Black Death figured heavily in the history of the Goddess because, "The Age of Chivalry was among the many casualties of the Plague. King Arthur's code of honor, which had ennobled earlier generations of aristocracy, was interred when 'knight' became synonymous with 'thug.' Fear of and respect for both clerical and secular authority slackened as familiarity with the Grim Reaper increased.…The decline in the moral status of both clergy and nobility in the eyes of the hard-working, over-taxed, church-going, middle and lower classes fanned dissent.…As the fourteenth century drew to a close, conditions were so bleak that most citizens were both physically debilitated and spiritually emaciated."

But by the middle of the fifteenth century, things began to change. The Hundred Years' War was over and a new spirit of economic growth spread over Europe and much of the rest of the world. Commerce grew and so did literacy rates. Reading and writing came into vogue once again, and with them came, "a new sense of self. The diffusion of books began to split the landmass of the Church into an archipelago of individual thinkers. Dirty bourgeois lucre, fertilizing the entwining skein of written words, produced the luxuriant tangle historians call the Renaissance.

"In 1454, Johannes Gutenberg received a patent on the printing press. The Chinese and the Koreans had used a similar device many centuries earlier, but Asian printers were hampered by the complexities of printing in ideographic script. Gutenberg needed little more than twenty-six bins, each one filled with a different letter of the alphabet. He could arrange a line of type in seconds and then rapidly pull sheet after sheet of paper covered with linear text."

The establishment class quickly grasped the new invention's potential for subversion, but it was too late; Pandora's Box had been opened. "Literacy rates, which had been steadily rising, suddenly exploded. The society in which this alphabetic adventure occurred, however, was completely knocked off its pins. No society had ever had to contend with the implications of so much literacy within such a short period of time. This factor...was the central cause of the Renaissance's agony and ecstasy."

This intellectual "rebirth" actually had begun in Italy in the middle fourteenth century and spread like ripples in a pond across Europe. A new wave of thinking was on the loose. "Invigorated by a new philosophy called Humanism, people began to see that they could make a difference....Perhaps Humanism should have been called 'Masculinism.' The leading proponents of Humanism did not advocate equality for women. It was a credo created by men, for men, and about men. Women of the era had to struggle with the Renaissance's predominantly macho themes, and also contend with the shift into their own left hemispheres as a result of *their* learning literacy.

"The principle of perspective was one of the key developments of Renaissance art. It is the visual equivalent of left-brained dualistic thinking. (Perspective is the illusion of depth on a flat surface. When a painting drawn in perspective is shown to people who are non-alphabet literate, they frequently cannot see the illusion. We who have been trained to read the alphabet are unaware that in order to read we focus our eyes slightly in front of a page of print. This skill is also indispensable in *seeing* a painting's perspectivist illusion.) Perspective accentuates the ability to stand outside what is being viewed and look back on it 'objectively.' All Western alphabet religions believe that God has a perspectivist point-of-view, looking down on His creation from on high. People in non-alphabetic traditions believe that the deity is both of and in the world. The deity isn't on the cloud—She *is* the cloud."

Perspective—but one of an entirely different nature—was one of the major reasons for the Reformation: a lack of female perspective within the Church. Ever since the anti-female policies of Pope Gregory VII in the 11th century, popes were unable to have women advisors on staff. "By banning women from any positions of authority within its corridors, the Vatican created the conditions for great mischief. In conjunction with a new invention that swiftly disseminated information (the first book printed in Rome appeared in 1469; by 1500 there were 41 printers) and changed the mind-set of a culture, conditions were in place for a debacle."

The reign of Pope Sixtus IV, which began in 1470, marks the beginning of the steep decline of papal authority and it ended during the reign of Clement VII on May 6, 1527 when Swiss, Dutch, German, and Spanish soldiers invaded Rome. The ensuing massacre, rape, fire, and plunder reached heights of man's inhumanity to itself not seen in more than a millennium. Many saw it as "divine retribution for the excesses of the previous eighty years. Taking into account the entire one thousand five hundred years of the church's existence, previous Church leaders had not exhibited behaviors so antithetical to the spirit of its founder for so many years...I propose that the sudden inundation of society by alphabet letters caused a dramatic increase in left-brain hunter-killer values throughout Europe, and diminution of right-brain values of life, kindness, equality, respect for nature, nurturing small children, protecting the meek and weak, and common sense. These trends became exaggerated in the wealthiest, all male, most literate segment of society—the papacy. In the Renaissance Vatican, gold, gain, pride, hubris, contests, and vainglory were held in the highest regard. The occasional papal mistress present during this period was not enough to counterbalance the extreme masculine ethos of the papal court. The absence of woman wisdom was an important factor to its resultant decline."

And so, given this background, the Reformation was inevitable, but its absence of female values is hard to explain. Calvin and Luther endured difficult childhoods which may explain their "dark views of human nature, but it does not explain why so many others embraced a religion of fear and trembling. Nor does it explain why the Reformation had no figures like Frances of Assisi, Hildegard, Abélard, Catherine of Siena, Meister Eckhart, Joan of Arc, or Jakob Böhme, or why there was not a single important female Protestant Reformer. The men who surrounded Calvin and Luther were, for the most part, very severe and dictatorial. Collectively, they instituted a very harsh patriarchy. Women were almost nonexistent in the organization and in the conduct of the new Protestant Church. Calvin explicitly prohibited women from baptizing.

Shlain maintains that what was sorely lacking in the Protestant Reformation was joy, love, mercy, laughter, and beauty. The Age of Chivalry in the eighth century, the devotion to Mary in the ninth, the mysticism of the tenth, the curiosity of the eleventh, the open-mindedness of the twelfth, the lustiness of the thirteenth, the individual ingenuity of the fourteenth, the Humanism of the fifteenth all stood in stark contrast to the sixteenth century's grim doctrine of abject helplessness.

Shlain holds that the Protestant Reformation was not a worldwide phenomenon. It only occurred in western European societies, and *only* in those cultures transformed by the art of printing. The Protestant Reformation was clearly not a return to the *content* of the New Testament; but, he suggested, a wrenching sociological shift wrought by a new information technology dependent on users being alphabet-literate. This, in turn, changed the collective perception of culture. The printing press made the Reformation's rigid and repressive self-discipline possible....Taken as a whole, the religious wars that wracked Europe in the 150 years after the printing press had transformed European culture and can be viewed as a sort of mass madness. They occurred only in those lands impacted by the printing press; the steeper the rise of literacy rates the more ferocious the religious wars were....Due to its exceedingly short learning curve, every society that had acquired alphabet literacy became violently self-destructive a short time afterward. This madness has been associated with virulent misogyny and spelled trouble for images, women's rights, Goddesses, and right-brained values...the process of writing and reading initially reinforced left-brain values to the detriment of right-brain values.

The evidence seems so overwhelming and worth remembering as we continue our review of where we are and how we got here concerning the current state of Man The Species (MTS). The next and last critical path on this 5,500-year runaway gallop into madness began during the century immediately preceding the twentieth. Like the alphabet, it at first seemed so positive—filled with great potential for the good of all humankind.

Chapter Three

The Main Problems For MTS

A. The Industrial Revolution—1850; Patriarchy's Last Gasp

According to some observers, Isaac Newton (1642-1727) best exemplifies the dramatic and sudden rise in rationality. Shlain explains it thusly: "His [Newton's] scientific discoveries convinced a majority of educated Europeans that the universe consisted of quantifiable objects and measurable forces obeying immutable laws." The late eighteenth century therefore became known as the period of Enlightenment. "These same thinkers deemed anything that could not be comprehended by reason was 'other'; by which they meant it was secondary, insignificant, not namable, less than real.

"For many men, women fell into the category of 'other.' 'Natural law' reinforced their conviction that they were 'naturally' superior to women....Thus European civilization passed from a patriarchal society based on laws handed down three thousand years earlier by a male deity into a new version of patriarchy founded on 'natural laws' discovered by male scientists....The Enlightenment and the scientific discoveries that underpinned it paved the way for a far greater drama—the Industrial

Revolution. This event had a profound effect on human relationships; comparable in impact only to the changes previously wrought by the development of agriculture and writing.

"The Industrial Revolution aggressively increased the sum total of tangible wealth and made possible many advances unimaginable in the preceding century. One technological marvel after another contributed to a rapid [*sic*] rising standard of living. But these innovations came with a price. The exploitation of children and a widening disparity between the rights and prerogatives of the sexes were just two of them."

A third was the separation of Man The Species (MTS) from his family—especially his children—more especially his sons.

B. Forgetting How to Be a Man—The Beginning of the End?

In the history of the development of civilization, the invention by John Kaye of the Flying Shuttle in the early part of the 19th century might prove the beginning of the end of the human male as a viable member of society. According to the *Encyclopedia Britannica*, Kaye's discovery marked the start of the Industrial Revolution, which for many observers has been the final straw in the self-destruction of MTS.

One such commentator has been Robert Bly, poet, mythologist, and author. In his book *Iron John*, Bly makes the point that MTS has forgotten how to be a man—a real man—not "mancho man," but one who is in "balance." Bly suggests that a real man (in other terms) is someone whose right and left brains are in relative balance—who is equally comfortable appreciating and blending with nature, changing diapers and cleaning house, playing ball with his and neighborhood children, lending a helping hand to the poor and dispossessed, reading a book, writing a letter to the editor, or standing when a woman enters a room. The trouble is these kinds of men are becoming harder and harder to find. Since the middle 19th century and especially since World Wars I and II, MTS has increasingly forgotten the "right" side of manhood while more and more embracing its "left" or hunter/killer characteristics.

According to Bly until the advent of the Industrial Revolution, Western civilization had done an acceptable job of helping the male youths of their day know how they should act when it was their turn to be the role models for society. How and where did it happen? Mostly on the farm. Before the nineteenth century A. D., the vast majority of people on the earth (*and* also those living in so-called civilized society) were farmers.

In his 1990 weekly PBS television series "A World of Ideas," Bill Moyers interviewed Robert Bly. The men's movement had just begun to get the attention of the national and international press. "A Gathering of Men" was and is a series of men's weekend retreats or workshops sponsored by Bly and several other prominent writers, philosophers, and academics. These get-togethers are designed to help men get in touch with their pain—the absence of fathers in their lives. Here are some relevant excerpts from that award-winning Moyers/Bly interview:

Bly: I think the grief that leads to the men's movement began, maybe a hundred and forty years ago, when the Industrial Revolution began. It sent the father out of the house to work.

Moyers: What impact did that have?

Bly: Well, we receive something physically from our father by standing close to him . . .

Moyers: Physically?

Bly: Yes. When we stand, physically, close to our father, something happens that can't be described in material terms. It gives the son a certain confidence, an awareness, a knowledge of what it is to be male. In ancient times you were always with your father. He taught you know to do things, he taught you how to farm, he taught you whatever it was he did. You learned from him.

Moyers: A kind of food.

Bly: Food, yes, food from your father's body. When the father went out of the house in the Industrial Revolution, that food ended. Today, the average American father spends ten minutes a day with a son, and half that time is spent in, "Clean up your room!" That's a favorite phrase of mine, I know it well.

The Industrial Revolution didn't harm the mother and daughter as much as it did the father and son. Mother and daughter have stood close to each other, and still stand close to each other. Daughters receive some kind of knowledge from their mothers of what it is to be a woman. They receive the knowledge of the female mode of feeling. The mother gets it from her grandmother, who got it from her grandmother; it goes all the way down. But now, I don't know, maybe that'll change too as mothers are going out to work.

After the Industrial Revolution, the male did not receive any knowledge from his father: knowledge of what the male mode of feeling is. And then, too, the old male initiators who used to work with younger men are not working anymore.

Moyers: Who were those "old initiators"?

Bly: Well, in traditional cultures, you aren't initiated by your father. You're initiated by older males; they might be friends of your father, or they could be uncles or grandfathers. They're the ones who used to initiate. But since they've disappeared, it falls on the father to do. But the father can't do it either, because he's at the office. You see the picture?

Later in the same interview.

Moyers: If we don't have the old initiations, what does happen with younger men?

Bly: As for my father, he didn't teach me much about the male mode of feeling, but he taught me something. But many men have no father at all, or the father left when they were two, or the father doesn't say anything, or the father doesn't talk well about feelings. It seems to be natural in the American male, not talking about feelings.

So then, how does the boy learn the male mode of feeling? He doesn't. It's a problem, and in the sixties, it came to a crisis, during the Vietnam War. The young men hadn't been helped by their fathers, and they were really betrayed by the older men during Vietnam. So, women would offer to initiate the young men; initiate them in wonderful things like respect for the earth, respect for feeling, and so on. That wasn't wrong at all, it's just that no one has helped them with the male mode of feeling.

Moyers: What's the chief difference, as you see it, between male feeling and female feeling?

Bly: A strong part of the woman's mode of feeling has to do with pain: moving towards pain, and helping to remove it. And there's also the pain of being devalued. I mean, woman's values have been rejected to this culture for over two thousand years, and women feel a strong pain in this devaluation. Men don't feel devalued quite that much. With men it's more an area of grief, as opposed to pain.

Later still in the same interview.

Moyers: Why do you think there's so much confusion today over what men are?

Bly: What models are we given in high school? John Wayne? All those models, they don't last past the age of thirty-two or so. Around thirty-five, men begin to realize that the images they were given of what a man is don't work. They don't work in their jobs, they don't work in a relationship, they don't work in the marriage; they don't work!

Moyers: So what happens when these high school images fade?

Bly: Well, I think there's a deep sense of failure, a sense that you're inadequate. The absence of the father standing next to the son, giving cellular significance—I don't know what you call it, cellular confidence, what we talked of earlier—when that's gone, you judge yourself a great deal more. It seems you're failing in your relationship. What was it Maggie Scarf said? The typical relationship in the United States involves the woman chasing the man to try to get him to talk more, and the man fleeing? But she doesn't chase him fast enough to really catch him, and he doesn't run away fast enough to really get away. That's the game that's played.

In a way, the man can't turn and face the woman, because without a clear sense of what it is to be a man, he can't stand and say, "Wait a minute, I know what I want in a relationship. It isn't exactly what you want, but let me tell you what it is." And he may fail. Since the woman knows what she wants in a relationship, the man again feels inadequate. I'd say the primary experience of the American man now is the experience of being inadequate. In work, you can't achieve what you want. You feel inadequate as a man because you don't have any close male friends, and you don't know why. You feel inadequate as a husband because your wife is always saying you don't talk about your feelings enough. And you don't know what your feelings are.

But, you know, men are not hiding their feelings from women. Men look down inside and they don't see anything in there. There's a feeling of numbness that, for men, comes early in life.

Moyers: Do you remember when you first began to get in contact with your feelings, as a man?

Bly: With men, there's some quality of grief. But men don't know what they're grieving about. It's as if the grief is impersonal with men. It's always present. You don't know if it's about the absence of the father, or if it's about all of the animals we were in touch with the millions of years we were hunters, and all the animals that died. It may be a grief that's in nature itself. You remember the Latin term *lacrimae rerum*, the "tears of things"? Men have lived for centuries out there, and they feel that terrific grief of nature and the out-of-doors and pine trees. There are certain little groves in England, if you walk in there, you'll burst into tears, because there's grief in nature.

Moyers: I grieve, but I don't write poems. What do I do about it?

Bly: I don't know that you have to *do* something with it. It's a choice, at any given second. You know, in a conversation there are little things, things you can turn, up or down....You can follow the grief downward in this way, or you can go upward in the American way. You can always tell an American on the streets of Europe, because he's always smiling.

Moyers: This is territory I'm not very competent to enter, but America never has really come to terms with the shadow of its past.

Bly: That's right.

Moyers: The Indians, the blacks.

Bly: We didn't mourn over the death of the Indians. I guess we did moderately well in mourning the Civil War, with Whitman and Lincoln. But after that, it's been a process of non-mourning. Alexandria Mitscherlich has written a book called *The Inability to Mourn* about the Germans after the Second World War. We're in the same situation. We have an inability to mourn. How can we have strong men or women if we can't go into grief at all?

During the remainder of the interview, Bly explains that he believes that the solution to the dysfunctional males in American society lies in the mentoring of the pubescent males by the elder males—the male mother, as he calls them.

Bly: "That's a man who does nurturing in a similar way as a woman, only he's not a woman. King Arthur acted that way for those young men."

Moyers: You talk about the old men giving the young men "Zeus energy." What do you mean, "Zeus energy"?

Bly: Well, the way the king is described in Greek mythology is through the image of Zeus. Zeus energy is authority that the male takes for the sake of the community. The American Indians in upstate New York, for example, had a strong chieftainship. The chief was chosen by women, and once the chief was chosen, he had to agree to give up all property. He had nothing that was his. And the authority that he had was for the sake of the community.

We don't have Zeus energy in corporations. With Exxon, you do things for money, for advancement, for power, for security. You're not doing anything for the sake of the community. They take their authority for the sake of the corporation, not for the sake of the community. In the corporation everybody is doing things for himself.

Moyers: Where did you get your Zeus energy?

Bly: I don't know if I have any Zeus energy. It could be I just have a big mouth, you know. That's always a possibility.

Moyers: No. I happen to know there are a lot of young writers and artists and students who look to you as a mentor.

Bly: Men didn't trust me until I was maybe 45 or 50. I don't know what that was, but I noticed it. And they were right not to trust me.

Moyers: Why?

Bly: If I don't have a connection with my father, where's my grounding? If I don't have a connection with grief, where's my grounding? So somewhere along the line, because of various disasters in my life, I must have gotten in touch with some sort of grief. Since then I've done a lot of work to try to maintain my connection with my father and deepen that.

Moyers: How can a 46-year-old man bond with his father after those long years of estrangement?

Bly: I don't have a good answer for that. But, well, here's a poem about my experience. Here's a poem about my attempt to thank him for the fathering he gave, even if it wasn't what I wanted.

There must have been
a fire, that nearly
blew out, or a large
soul inadequately
feathered, who became
cold and angered.
Some four-year-old boy
in you, chilled by
your mother, misprized
by your father, said
"I will defy. I will win
anyway, I will show them."
When Alice's well-off sister
Offered to take your two
boys during the Depression
you said it again.
Now you speak the defiant
words to death.
This four-year-old
old man in you does
as he likes: he likes
to stay alive.
Through him you
get revenge,
persist, endure,
overlive, overwhelm,
get on top.
You gave me
this, and I do
not refuse it.
It is
in me.

So I realized, then, that my father gave me this, "I will defy, I will win." It's not the gift I wanted, but it was a gift. My other father was Yeats. He was my male mother. He wasn't alive, but your mentor doesn't have to be alive. Does that make sense?

Moyers: What does a male mother do that the father doesn't do?

Bly: The father cannot really do the initiation with his son because there's too much tension. They're both interested in the same woman, and that's a problem. When men recognize their fathers can't do it, and that the initiators are gone...there's no one to welcome the young man into the male world. Young men are angry about that.

When you're looking at a gang, you're seeing young males who have no older men to welcome them into the male world. They're trying desperately to do it themselves. They're trying to teach each other what courage is, how much pain you should endure, what a cause is. They're trying to do it, but it doesn't work, because young males cannot initiate each other. But they're angry at the absence of the older males who are not doing that. When this group of old males initiators disappears, everything falls on the father. The father's supposed to do everything. When young men realize their father could have done that, they begin to think of the things their father did try to do. Oftentimes, they're touched, they weep when they think of the possibilities.

Moyers: So when the older men—

Bly: Fathers are supposed to keep us alive to the age of 17, make sure we don't get eaten by ants, or packs of wild dogs. Fathers were never intended to initiate sons.

Moyers: But what happens when the father is gone? In America today, so often it's just a single mother who is left to do it, the initiation, and...

Bly: That's right, and women try very hard. They try very hard with this, but it's hopeless. A woman can bring the boy from being a fetus to being a boy, but she can't move him from being a boy to being a man. Only other men can do that . . .

As we have just observed, Moyers and Bly discussed several problems all of us see reverberating through modern society. To review, they were:

1. The Industrial Revolution became the death knell for the tradition male role in society since the beginning of mankind's agricultural societies some 5-10,000 years ago.
2. The usually unspoken grief of the modern male at what he sees when he looks inside himself—the absence of the "male mode of feeling."
3. The lack of modern-day male role models.
4. The terror at the hollowness the modern male knows is himself, and the plain reality that he doesn't know where to turn for a solution.
5. The absence of "male mothers" who have experienced real grief and found their grounding—the unwillingness of the older males to be the initiators of the new young men.

These issues form the core of the problems we must address in order to provide a comprehensive discussion for the future of MTS in western society, and especially these United States. As we will soon see, the majority of the symptoms of modern societal malaise, which I first mentioned at the beginning of Chapter One, have their genesis in one or more of the issues covered above by Moyers and Bly.

However, the principle building block of our ongoing discourse on this subject has to be a recognition and acceptance by the reader of the significance of the change in behavior the Industrial Revolution brought to western civilization. I claim that the farm was the last place men and women needed each other on a survival level, and the disappearance of that mutual interdependence has caused irreparable damage to western civilization. Without that common agreement, everything I say from this point forward would be of questionable value. Nevertheless, convinced that I have sufficiently made that case, I will now proceed to address the other societal ills or problems which I believe play an important—albethey somewhat less weighty, save one—role in this entire discussion.

C. Denial and Its Many Forms

An example of the genius of modern mankind is our ability to develop an amazing menu of alternatives to being with ourselves. As a consequence, we're becoming less interesting to ourselves and often need an outside sedative to be comfortable within our own skin. In city and suburban life where alienation, loneliness, and boredom pervade the very fabric of daily life, our survival requires that we re-discover the ability to make ourselves interesting to ourselves. If we fail, our only alternative is denial. Our institutions no longer provide meaningful answers for complex questions of the day insofar as they affect common man and woman. As a result many of us are on our way to dying slowly; many more are already partially dead but survival instincts programmed for millions of years allow us to endure and ignore much that is unpleasant. It's easier to deny the problems of society than to address them directly.

Part of the problem Male The Species (MTS) has had with respect to an understanding of his changing role in modern society has been—until the last decade or so—the inclination for all of society to pretend nothing was wrong—aka denial. An essential common denominator of the problems articulated by Bly and Moyers (in their PBS interview) was the societal denial factor which "enabled" (more psycho-babble) such "symptoms" to continue and grow and burrow into the heart of western civilization.

Nonetheless, in 1990 Bly's ideas were—at that time—almost ground-breaking. The almost hysterical controversy which greeted his book *Iron John* —by both men and women groups—continues to this day. Instead of addressing the issues the book raised, many groups persist in vilifying the messenger or males as a group—especially white Anglo-Saxon Protestant (WASP) males. Many groups who profess to advance women's role in society persist in the notion of achieving their ends at the expense of MTS. "If there's a cultural problem, a man or a group of men must have caused it; they've been in charge since the beginning of recorded time," has often been the stock-in-trade rallying-cry of such groups. Because they're "stuck" ideologically, it's almost impossible for these well-intentioned organizations to embrace the possibility that all of society played a part in the creation of MTS' current confusion about what his role should be. A wise person once wrote: "There are none so blind as those who will not see."

For MTS, the many forms of denial have been and continue to be almost limitless in number and creativity. At first—in the middle and late 19th century—MTS reacted with an attitude like: "Problem? What problem? I don't see any problem." That was quickly followed by (in the early 20th century) variations on the same theme: "What our friend Joe needs is a good woman or a good butt-kicking or to grow up or for his parents to quit babying him or for him to join the Marines (any branch of the military would do) and find out what life's really all about." For much of American society these attitudes about how to cure the ills of MTS remained static up until the beginning of the Vietnam War. After that, we seemed to divide into two major camps: (1) "Why don't you just leave Fred alone and let him have some space—he'll figure it out?" or "Who the hell died and left you in charge? What makes you think you're so smart?"; (2) "He's nothing but a no good, pinko communist or socialist. He, Jane Fonda, and all their friends should just pack up and leave the good old U.S.of A. I hear Charles de Gaulle or Ho Chi Min would welcome them with open arms!"

However, with the end of the Vietnam War and the mass confusion that followed during the middle and late seventies, the toll on American society grew exponentially each month the problem went un-addressed. Today, significant numbers of "Boomers" and the "Gen-Xers" have suddenly come to the conclusion that something really and truly is wrong with our society, but their solution was (and in some cases still is) to blame MTS. Then along came Gail Sheehy and Dr. Warren Farrell and Dr. Sam Keen (to name a few) who made the case that all society—not just the male—had a significant hand in creating our present societal crisis about the role of MTS. That said, the psycho-babble *de jour* seems predisposed to re-visit the ills of society through "advocacy" research. A new book *How We're Ruining Our Boys* by Gail Sheehy finally confronts the fact that both young men *and* women are victims of our confused society; it begins in the nation's kindergarten and elementary schools. The lessons should be clear: When we single out one group for punishment, all civilization suffers. Witch-hunting by any other name is still witch-hunting.

Nevertheless, while the academic and literary community debate whom to blame, the problems persist and so does our collective denial. The real issues still appear too difficult and polarizing to allow meaningful societal discussion. So western civilization falls back on tried-and-true kinds of group denial—and a few new ones as well.

1. Religion:

First of all, as most of you have concluded by now, I'm an agnostic, but I'd love to see God in action. However, I could also accept what I will call "The Unknown God." There is a realm of unknown; the great unknown has not shown me any suggestion of order. It has shown me unbelievable chaos and unfairness and what havoc nature can wreak. As long as we have an unknown, we can't preclude any possibilities. We don't know where and how the universe started and why. So we have this magnificent and exciting unknown and many people call it God. If we can agree to call that The Unknown God, that's fine with me.

Beyond that I don't think I could agree; I'd have to see better evidence than I have so far that there is an all-knowing, all-powerful, benevolent force I could agree to call God. So in those terms, I'm an agnostic which means—among other things—I choose to give little weight to the latest religious fads—like "New Ageism" or "Oneism"—to explain the universe.

What I know for certain is there's a huge atmosphere in space dotted with clusters of stars and planets. There's also many unproven theories about how this planet arrived, and that each of us is comprised of some unique mixture of gases. Trouble is there's no reason to think mankind is anything special other than something which evolved arbitrarily from other gases. We don't know really why we're here or whether there is any "why" we're here; but here we are.

I accept the fact that I am here and have certain needs. I also know that while I'm here, it's much better to feel good and have enough food and comfortable shelter. The absence of pain feels much better than the presence of pain itself. To me, that's a truth I can embrace.

As I said earlier, I'd love to see God in action sometime. I've been on this earth a lot of years, and I'd be happy to see a sign of some prime mover's existence. I haven't seen any yet—that I know of—but I've seen a lot of the other side—the negative side—of what so many people like to call God. Religion strikes me as a heroic effort by men and women to order society so they can be happy. I don't object to people vectoring into fantasy to find happiness; it's another type of narcotic and probably one of the least objectionable. With religion, you're trading whatever hardships there are here on earth for the belief that it's all going to be beautiful in the next world; it means that mankind has found a narcotic that places it in a sort of a survival-status without necessarily achieving the natural joy and happiness that is life-enhancing and non-destructive to all life. By promising eternal happiness, religion over the past five millennia has had a great narcotic-like effect on the masses.

For the sake of this component of our discussion, let's say I agree with Marx in his definition of religion as being the opiate of the masses. But unlike that now discredited 19th century Russian philosopher, I also believe religion can have a beneficial value in modern society because it soothes the wild beast in many of us. Other than the special ethnic situations where there has been an ongoing history of group hatred, I haven't seen any current religious leaders successfully create the kind of fanaticism we've seen in the previous 5,000 years. I think that 19th and 20th century science and technology has moved us away from that possibility—another example of how the industrial revolution has re-defined society.

Also, a government granting so-called freedom of religion to disparate religious groups is a bloodless way of establishing control over them. It helps create cohesiveness and order—leaders can gather taxes, encourage industriousness, and gain support for wars. So there are a number of practical control-uses of religion for modern government leaders. I'm not against that *and* I'm not for it. Day-to-day living can be brutal; so having an opiate or being able to partake of that opiate is not necessarily a bad thing.

Sometimes I'm envious of believers because I think there are many aspects of their mindset that is healthful—a natural narcotic much like joy or happiness. However, there's another definition I have developed for religion; it's called *interimation*—something people can do "in the interim" while trying to figure out what the highest and best use their being may have.

Some of us—too many unfortunately—never find the answer to the question of our highest and best use; we're too busy trying to survive. We could say that good mating and love is the most acceptable narcotic we have, if we chose to term that a narcotic. Nevertheless, cultures the world over during the past 5,000 years have primarily looked to religion (Zen, Buddhism, Hinduism, Christianity, or Judaism to name but a few) to find an explanation for their relationship to the universe and, even more importantly to believers, what happens after death—an essential element of this particular opiate for the masses. However, another positive aspect of religion is that in many cases it does get people to thinking. It appears that western men and women are thinking a lot these days about their belief systems.

Recently, a new religion has begun to evolve; it's especially evident in the arts. It's what I call *neo-reality*. Spinoza was one of its first theorists as were the Zen Buddhists. I see America entering this world of neo-reality; a reality that has some mystery and excitement but which attempts to see the world realistically without the hypnosis and mind control of institutional religion. This new religion embraces the notion of spiritually in individuals and finds mystery and excitement in everyday life. All each of us has for sure is everyday life, and if we do not find value and mystery in everyday life, we're postponing happiness—a happiness that could sustain us in the present. I think we have to find our moment-to-moment *opiation* in the enjoyment of the moment. No matter how it's packaged, religion is still an opiate—a form of denial.

I find that people who claim to have found God live in a kind of a bubble. There's a whole area of consciousness they don't have to worry about—a whole anxiety absent from their reality. They are believers; they respond well to hypnosis and find its benefits valuable. They derive satisfaction from being part of something—a blessing the person who isn't prone to being hypnotized can never understand. That may be a good thing, especially in light of the fact that day-to-day living is like living alone somewhere in the middle of the desert—it's difficult and filled with challenges we each must confront alone on a daily basis. Of course, people can be made to do things by suggestion under hypnosis. And we've seen in the past that when a group or an individual can control the minds of others, there's a potential benefit *and* danger.

Immediately preceding the Reformation, the Catholic Church was the only religion in western civilization. Historically, since then, institutional religion has either adapted to society or become irrelevant. Since the Reformation, different groups have splintered away from the Church so now we have hundreds of religious groups changing and forming. Today, we see all institutional religions wrestling with the great problems of birth control, abortion, women priests, homosexuality, situational ethics caused by new technology breakthroughs in biology, physics, astrology, and genome engineering (the list is virtually endless). They don't have all the answers, so we don't really have a constant form and role for religion.

We have great changes and a society which is in the process of re-defining the role religion should play in the lives of humankind. Western civilization and America in particular is in the process of deep (I use the word "deep" because in most instances this process is taking place at a subconscious or unconscious level because to speak of it is too frightening for too many people) contemplation and inarticulated thought about the future of religion. For many, that process has produced a unspoken movement toward meditation because there just doesn't seem to be enough empirical data for a person to sit down and logically develop a theological plan for his/her own peace and happiness. Meditation is easier to understand by western humankind. The more knowledge we have about why the institutional paradigms no longer seem to work, the more chance we have of obtaining a true understanding of the dynamic of silent contemplation instead of retreating into the anesthesia of escape from the explosion of new knowledge, ideas, and technology. So while this process plays itself out in the fullness of time, a vacuum has been created. Wherever a vacuum exists, it is a law of nature that something will rush in to fill it. Enter other forms of societal sedation that require little or no thought and are much less dangerous—or so it is believed by their disciples.

2. The New Religion—Entertainment:

Today, although much of western society retains the outward appearances and infrastructures of institutional religion, in many respects that opiate has been replaced. If you doubt me, look closely at what people are doing. They stand three and four hours at public stadiums, waiting to buy a ticket to a movie, sporting event, or rock concert. Tell me if that's not a form of religion—a narcotic, an escape from reality? Do you see anyone standing three and four hours to buy a ticket to the next choir practice or for the next Saturday synagogue or Sunday church services. When people line up for hours to get tickets to watch the entertainment gods, we know something is going on.

The actual movie, game, or concert is just that; but because of the unusual enthusiasm of those willing to sacrifice so much, we know something more is at work from a societal perspective. Escape which contains a love interest, an aspect of nourishing, or a seed-strengthening component are areas of primary interest for most humans. Those are the things people will get up from the couch and leave their house to enjoy or pursue. There's an emotional involvement—an almost hypnotic one—back to a kind of religious zeal. Simultaneously, there's a conscious effort by many people in western civilization—overtly or subconsciously—to reject the religious teachings of the '50s or before. And having found little comfort or security in modern institutional religion, great numbers of people in the so-called advanced societies of this planet have now embraced another form of denial—the Narcotic of Entertainment: movies, television, theater, sports, and, more recently, the Internet. With the proliferation of Web sites and e-everything from books to commerce to religion, all forms of escape are as available as your TV or computer screen. These more recent forms of mind control and societal escape have, for great numbers of people in western culture, replaced the institutional religions as the center of their daily lives. Far too many of us now live only for their soap operas or World Wide Wrestling (WWF) or The Oprah Winfrey Show or the next Harry Potter book or *Star Wars* or who's going to be world champion in soccer, football, basketball or baseball—all available on your nearest computer or TV monitor.

Few of members of modern society—especially MTS—seem to comprehend the real dynamic at work, i.e. that they've become vicarious participants in the game of life—that the watching of football, baseball, or tennis for hours robs them of human relationships—that there are things they could be doing with their significant other which would bring joy to both, like taking a walk by the beach or doing the family grocery shopping together or just sitting down and having a conversation about their own thoughts; better yet, getting in touch with their own thoughts. There is so much more to enjoy in this life than simply being entertained. Where is their awareness that what they are doing is conditioned by their environment and may not be giving them qualitative gratification but more of a narcotic or novocaine from life—an escape from their own happiness? They certainly don't get much insightful guidance from institutional religion—the clergy of which (in most instances) are well-intentioned males.

To curry favor with their diminishing flocks, many clerics have recently taken to leading their parish in prayers for the success of a local professional sports team or erecting their own Web site where they attempt to maintain the fiction that they can become all things to all people. Despite these futile and desperate attempts to reverse the tidal wave of preoccupation with what can be seen and heard by mindlessly viewing a television or computer monitor, MTS (along with the rest of society) must face reality.

At the beginning of the third millennium, the Era of Mass Communications (EMC) has basically replaced the Industrial Revolution as the newest and most influential phenomenon molding society—and in ways never before witnessed on this planet and with ramifications of which most of us would never even dare to dream.

3. The Mass Communications Revolution:

Back around the turn of the 20th century, western mankind was just beginning to embrace the concept of cities as a potential force for good in society—a force capable of providing benefits to civilization more than sufficient to compensate for the permanent loss of the family farm and its intrinsic positive virtues. Simultaneously, two discoveries were just reaching adolescence: electricity and photography. And by the middle of the new century, these inventions had led to the development of radio, television, movies, the recording industry, and the computer— mass communications had arrived.

At the epicenter of this societal earthquake stands Hollywood—one of the two main gatekeepers of modern civilization and *the* icon community for the entertainment and mass communications industry. Still, the past 50 years' events have even been moving too fast for even the "best and the brightest" on either coast; most academics and self-proclaimed experts agree: There's been insufficient time to digest and comprehend the full range of consequences of these new communication systems. In the past, the slower the induction of knowledge, the more humankind's ability to assimilate and make sense of it. Absent that, mass confusion follows—especially when Hollywood, purposely or accidentally, controls so much of what we read, hear, and view. "Power corrupts; absolute power corrupts absolutely."

Contrary to the protestations of innocence by the communications industry, we do follow their lead in societal mores because they have the bully pulpit—they didn't ask for it, but they do have it. Whether they want it or not, they set the cultural agenda because they are the gatekeepers of what we read, see, and hear.

The first word which comes to mind when someone mentions Hollywood is "artificial." Truth is the first casualty of what they do. Stories about real people doing well and fulfilling their dreams have little value in their product line. Vast majorities of the western world, apparently, want to vicariously overcome evil, find hope, or a wonderful moment of passion and true love. Hollywood lives and breathes these invented crises, problems, villains, heroes, and solutions. In the past 75 years, we've been so bombarded with entertainment's shallow version of life that we've come to accept those versions as truth.

Modern society is like the prisoner whose captors drive him crazy with continuous drops of water falling on his head. Little by little, we've lost our way and we're not sure anymore of how we're supposed to act. Since growing numbers of us no longer accept institutional religion as a valid resource for morality in times of trouble or disorientation, we turn back to Hollywood or even the "Big Apple" (New York City)— surely they can tell us what to be, what love is, how husbands and wives should act, what acceptable behavior is and what is not. But since they don't possess any more wisdom than the rest of us (often less), the result is chaos.

No one seems to have a solution that resonates with a majority of the "boomer" generation or the "Gen Xers" and younger. The proof can be found in the turmoil of our cities—now the heartbeat of all western civilization. Effective interaction between citizens is at a new low. Fresh levels of violence break out daily around the world like fresh cases of the Plague—violence that would heretofore been thought impossible (**example:** the gang rape in New York City of innocent women while passersby merely watched and recorded the incident on their own TV cameras; **example:** the wanton hooliganism at sporting or entertainment events in all corners of the planet; **example:** teenagers bludgeoning migrants). Real law and order has become a fiction— replaced by a tenuous truce supported by protected enclaves, high retaining walls, and a proliferation of security guards. Even schools and libraries have to maintain a strong security presence so their patrons can have peace of mind.

Mass communications may have brought new vistas of instant information to greater numbers of people, but it hasn't brought them happiness; it hasn't brought them self-esteem, and it hasn't brought them an understanding of themselves. Even if they could find happiness on the Internet, most people (MTS especially) wouldn't recognize the road to happiness if they tripped over it. Like the birds in *Jonathon Livingston Seagull*, it's much more comfortable to keep making the same mistakes as the rest of society, even if they don't bring happiness. Burying oneself in work or career is a whole lot safer than trying to "think outside the box" of conventional wisdom.

4. Status:

For most of us, life is a lonely state. It comes with no road map, no operating instructions. Mostly we're left to guessing about which is the correct path in any given situation. It's so comforting when any of us read or hear others who have similar backgrounds and seem to have found answers to life's many puzzlements. This has especially been the case for MTS since the dawn of the Industrial Revolution. It seemed obvious to many then—as it does now—that what MTS was supposed to do was exchange his role as chief worker and organizer of the farming operations for a similar role in the industrial community. Depending on his particular talents and skills, a male would be performing the same basic functions, just within a different environment. And the rewards for those who made the adjustment and "bought into" this new role for MTS seemed almost too good to be true. The money poured in and he could buy his family a new home and furniture and cars and clothes and a college education and travels around the world and the list never seemed to end.

But, just as in the song by Peggy Lee, MTS found himself asking, "Is that all there is?" He'd wake up one day at age 50 or 60 and discover that his children basically saw him as a money machine and little else. He wasn't really a part of their lives because he never had been; he'd mostly been at work or sleeping or telling them to "clean their rooms." His wife would spend her days at the "club" playing golf or bridge or raising money for some important cause and he was alone...still. The myth was—and remains so in the lives of too many males—that all he had to do to fulfill his portion of the social contract was to "bring home the bacon." But at age 50 or 60 (if they were lucky enough to have their naïveté go unchallenged for that long), males may find—to their great shock and disillusionment—that their own family sees them as having made only one meaningful contribution to their lives. Hurt and confused, MTS huddles with friends. Solution? Have an affair or hang out with the guys. (Having an affair has always been an option for MTS—no matter the point in time—3,000 BC or 2000 AD. In the main, males [and females] who follow that path eventually realize it leads nowhere. In the end, they're still alone, but now they've traded away their self-esteem with little or nothing to show for it except—in most cases—a broken home and an empty checkbook.)

"Hanging out with the guys" usually meant joining some kind of organization—Kiwanis, Lion's Club, Rotary, Chamber of Commerce. "Joining" usually meant having to contribute in some measurable way. That meant trading added duties and responsibilities in exchange for recognition—but now it would be recognition by his peers. Status. Title or power or both. Now there's something to really think about— something to give MTS a new lease on life and resurrect those long forgotten "seed-carrier" inclinations.

Remember back in Chapter Two when we talked about how in modern society that MTS' seed-carrier instinct had metamorphosed itself into the appearance of "doing well?" If it looked as if a particular member of MTS were doing well, then he became all the more "potent" in the eyes of the world—to both males and females of all ages (*status*, the magical 20th century elixir)! To much of the western world, it's "to die for." As a rule, status from the rest of the world comes to movie stars, politicians, certain kinds of athletes and entertainers, and lately to high-profile businessmen like Donald Trump or Bill Gates. But when I talk to males who have this so-called "status," they're not happy.

Many say they'd rather just have the money. Those with money say they'd rather have the status, and, not surprisingly, if they have status *and* money, those males say they would rather be a great archaeologist (or whatever). The human condition never seems to allow contentment. There's always somebody with a larger net worth, a bigger airplane, more power; the status game is a no-win game.

I was once at a dinner party where one of the men was worth about $400,000,000. Somebody else there also had a lot of money, and the conversation turned to the new house the second guy was building and the kind of yacht he was building and kind of airplane he was negotiating to buy. The wealthier of the two had sold his yacht and still had the flame for more status. He had also built a house with a swimming pool that stretched between the inside and outside of his new estate. It cost about $20,000,000 and he was receiving homage from the others at the party. Some of them suggested they were entitled to more homage than these rich guys because their company was employing thousands of people in Mexico. Some at the party agreed, but in the end, the vast majority huddled around the two multi-millionaires trying to "one-up" each other in a sort of in-person "Tales of the Rich and Famous."

Gail Sheehy also observed this very same phenomenon in her book *Understanding Men' Passages* when she wrote about the "Dominant Male Model." So for too many members of MTS, status in certain quarters is based on the size of the toys, and other times it's about political or economic power. But it's always about winning. Joseph Kennedy (father of the entire Massachusetts Kennedy Clan) personified this belief system way back in the late '50s, and drilled that concept into the minds and hearts of his offspring—especially his sons: *Status* is for winners!

5. The Need For Icons:

Take the case of Bill Gates. He's become an international icon—a symbol of wealth and power and hard work and the American entrepreneurial spirit. That's an important component of any icon for MTS. It's not enough that they be rich or powerful or both, they also have to embody some aspect of the American dream or even a more universal vision like international free market capitalism. The idea that anyone can start with nothing and by using a little foresight and a lot of hard work mixed with a dash of good fortune, anything's possible.

However, Gates' icon status is confined to certain limited circles of interest. Many people could care less about him or Microsoft or the world of business. Some even despise him because they see him as the embodiment of capitalistic imperialism—running around the globe buying or crushing smaller, weaker competitors in order to dominate an industry. Witness the fact that the U.S. Federal government has taken Microsoft to court, trying to break them up and destroy their perceived stranglehold on international software markets. According to the Clinton administration, Microsoft is "an insidious economic force" running unchecked throughout the marketplaces of the world because of the competitive advantages it has established for itself and its consumers by shear force of vertical and horizontal integration.

Bill Gates will always be a rich man, but his icon status may have run its course. If that's true, someone else will take his place. Like all segments of modern society, the business world needs its icons. The same dynamic is at work for a male's football, basketball, or baseball team; likewise for movie, TV, and rock stars. Icons represent hope and power, especially for MTS. A male icon is a living symbol of seed strengthening or seed carrying. If a 21st century male can discover an icon with whom he can identify, vicariously his own seed-carrier status has been strengthened and enhanced.

However, that's not the case for most people in *Who's Who* or *The Blue Book* as the "old money" people at the country club used to call it. Such men and women were raised not to be celebrities; they simply made significant accomplishments to society or had been wealthy or sometimes both. Nevertheless, for the better part of two-hundred years, these were the people who formed the silent backbone of our society. These were the people who shunned fame or seeing their name in the newspaper, saved their money, raised their families, and tried to pass on the good values given them by their parents and grandparents. There still are members of society (especially MTS) who appreciate someone with a good marriage and whose children have gone to college or raised themselves up by their bootstraps and done well. They're the real heroes or icons nobody knows about—the quiet ones who get virtually no press but the sum total of their life's work adds up to *status for others*, not themselves.

But in the last 40 years, icons must be part of the celebrity class to have status and standing. Being rich or smart or successful is not enough. Jackie Kennedy and Princess Diana had status; Michael Jordan has status. Donald Trump has status; even Regis Philbin has a certain amount of status—at least for the moment.

Because of television, the Internet, and the mass communications world we live in today, status and fame must be part of the same package. But mostly, they come and go relatively quickly. Modern society, especially as we enter the new millenium, has learned that *status* has no real staying power when it comes to evaluating the quality of another human. That's especially true for MTS. Being President of the United States or achieving high office in a corporation, or receiving a Pulitzer Prize means nothing; those achievements in and of themselves have no lasting *status*. The real and lasting status only comes (or doesn't) afterwards. It depends upon the individual—what they do with such high office. They could be a hero or a goat.

So what does have lasting status?

6. Materialism—All That's Left:

Frustrated with our inability to find lasting celebrities, we've now entered a period where smaller and smaller groups in society have decided they need their own status figure—their own icon. If you're a victim of a terminal disease or just love riding with your bike club, Lance Armstrong carries your torch. If you're a starving artist or writer and especially if you're a single, divorced mother, J. K. Rowling is your hero. If you're a minority and feel shunned by the establishment or just love golf, Tiger Woods connects with you. And if you're a male and feel as if society has turned a deaf ear to your needs and pain, Robert Bly or Joseph Campbell or Warren Farrell may be someone after whom to model your life. Some historians or literary critics think Samuel Clemens was someone special, others give special recognition to Shakespeare or Steinbeck. Economists might think Samuelson or Laffer made significant contributions in these fields. But all these opinions are based on a specific talent and reputation within a specialized frame of reference.

The proliferation of groups and their chosen status symbols continues almost unabated. But it's extremely difficult to find that one natural, universal icon we once enjoyed like with a General Eisenhower or Eleanor Roosevelt, both of whom had at least one major accomplishment for the betterment of all humankind to his/her name and was revered and respected around the world by friend and foe alike. Mother Theresa or Muhammad Ali come to mind as viable examples of lasting celebrities or icons of the past decade, but they're the notable exceptions.

Mostly, the growth of the icon class has paralleled that of mass communications and the world's population. From about the beginning of the Korean War, the number of people on this planet has risen from 4 billion to 6 billion—a 50 percent increase. That's roughly the same time period in which communications has changed from one dominated by the written word to one driven by images—visual images laser-beamed around the world at the speed of light into people's living rooms, palaces, and cold-water shacks. Visual communications are the rule today through the medium of television and the Internet; the written word is largely a secondary means of communication— newspapers, books, handwritten letters.

In many ways, western civilization has already begun a return to its pre-historic roots of more than 6,000 years ago—a more populist approach. So-called early civilized humankind (*circa* 3,000 BC) gave themselves special names or titles to elevate one over another. That led to the concept of royalty, one society doesn't recognize anymore.

We're now experiencing a time where most of the middle class doesn't see anyone to whom they should give much special deference— all humankind has feet of clay. If someone other than a member of the "business class" meets Bill Gates in the airport, they feel they can talk to him just as well as they could anyone else. So the sashes of royalty and insignia and titles and status are growing into obscurity, and as they leave, the next levels of societal gradation become the measuring rods (i.e., how beautiful is your wife, how many jewels she has, the house, the car). Materialism has replaced morality as the basis for value judgments about each other—our whole basis of judging "success." I call this concept *neo-realism* because it too is as hollow as those which have preceded it.

7. A New Paganism:

But something else is taking place at the same time—the (so-called) re-paganization of society and even more confusion for MTS. In our 21st century version of this old abstraction (a belief in non-monotheism), we are inadvertently returning to the habits of pre-historic culture—the days of multiple gods and goddesses. As we read earlier, such cultures had the cult God of war, the cult God of rain, and a God of thunder; they were broken up into twenty or thirty or more pagan Gods and idols from that. And, these Gods and Goddesses lived and thrived together.

It's interesting to see how history repeats itself. We now have the Gods of golf, we have the Gods of boxing. Oprah Winfrey has become a cult Goddess for great numbers of women. Margaret Thacher, Golda Meir, and Princess Grace of Monico (a.k.a. Grace Kelly of Hollywood celebrity status) were also Goddesses of a kind from our more recent 20th century. Princess Diana and Mother Theresa became modern living Goddesses (against their will), and remain so in many minds and hearts yet today, despite their nearly simultaneous deaths. When was the last time before 1997 that the world stopped everything it was doing and mourned the death of two females within a one-week period?

John F. Kennedy, Martin Luther King, Robert Kennedy, John Denver, and John F. Kennedy, Jr. were the last males to enjoy such universal appeal. A lot has changed in the world of MTS since 1963—Vietnam; Watergate; innumerable Mid-East-related atrocities around the world; the rise of Islamic Fundamentalism and its resultant international terrorism; the collapse of: the USSR, the Berlin Wall, and Yugoslavia; Desert Storm; Bill Clinton; and the U. S. elections of 2000—each another male-dominated public folly. Muhammad Ali or Ronald Reagan most likely will be the next member of MTS to stir worldwide sorrow at his passing—perhaps Bishop Butu from South Africa as well—but they're an ever-decreasing minority. Are we witnessing a trend?

Look at the modern commercials, movies, television, magazines, and other forms of mass communication. Women are smart, MTS is stupid. Children are wonderful, but MTS doesn't know anything; even his children have to set him straight about what cars to buy, where to get good information about planning a vacation, or how to brush his teeth. There's little left which celebrates manhood. MTS finds himself on the defensive on virtually all fronts—in the business world, at home, and in our institutions. The drumbeat is hard to ignore. So now MTS seeks answers—answers chanted in a constant barrage from our mass communications culture: "Be more nurturing!"

For most of MTS that means they should get more in touch with their feminine nature—their nurturing persona—but they have no idea how. Religion has no answers, neither do heroic deeds nor great accomplishments. So they retreat into working harder and longer hours, or the pursuit of more status (anywhere he can get it), or escape—maybe one (any one) will help him regain his lost manhood. "Besides," they tell themselves, "now females are going to get even for misdeeds I had nothing to do with; western society doesn't care anymore about my problems. Just shut-up and make your alimony or child-support payments on time!"

Maybe the 19th century philosopher Friederich Nietzsche was right. Maybe *Nihilism* is the answer. Why not just live for the moment? Why not create our own gods—our own reality?

According to the *Encyclopedia Britannica*, "In his mature writings Nietzsche was preoccupied by the origin and function of values in human life. If, as he believed, life neither possesses nor lacks intrinsic value and yet is always being evaluated, then such evaluations can usefully be read as symptoms of the condition of the evaluator. He was especially interested, therefore, in a probing analysis and evaluation of the fundamental cultural values of Western philosophy, religion, and morality, which he characterized as expressions of the ascetic ideal.

"The ascetic ideal is born when suffering becomes endowed with ultimate significance. According to Nietzsche the Judeo-Christian tradition, for example, made suffering tolerable by interpreting it as God's intention and as an occasion for atonement. Christianity, accordingly, owed its triumph to the flattering doctrine of personal immortality, that is, to the conceit that each individual's life and death have cosmic significance. Similarly, traditional philosophy expressed the ascetic ideal when it privileged soul over body, mind over senses, duty over desire, reality over appearance, the timeless over the temporal. While Christianity promised salvation for the sinner who repents, philosophy held out hope for salvation, albeit secular, for its sages. Common to traditional religion and philosophy was the unstated but powerful motivating assumption that existence requires explanation, justification, or expiation. Both denigrated experience in favor of some other, 'true' world. Both may be read as symptoms of a declining life, or life in distress."

Clearly, Nietzsche didn't have all the answers, either. Such issues do not lend themselves to easy solutions. The essence of what we're talking about here is how best to relate to the rest of the world while also finding emotional and physical happiness, absent artificial stimuli. I call such activities "narcotics" because too often people use them to find what—at the time—seems like happiness (alcohol, drugs, materialism, etc., a.k.a. *fool's happiness*). The truth is such deeds diminish the individual in the long run and create even more anguish. We can look and find that much of the world's problems have their genesis in unhappy people displacing their anger through war and hate and an absence of love. We can trace most of the obsessive activities of mankind to an absence of balance and contentment. You don't find a Hitler and a Mussolini and Napoleon and Caesar taking root in a balanced and happy person.

8. Self-Destructive Behavior:

Nietzsche beckons and when people perceive an absence of hope in religion, entertainment, materialism, or new forms of worship, many turn to self-destructive activities—opiates that trick their mind and body. These delusions come in many forms—over and under-eating, bulimia, hard and soft narcotics, nymphomania, alcohol, gambling, and the like. In their hearts, most participants know such activities are palliatives lacking day-to-day balance. Like an injection (sometimes they actually are), each behavior provides momentary pleasure or gratification, but only brief over the long-term. Like many others, Nietzsche's ideas are better on paper than in real life. For most members of MTS in the 21st century, *Nihilism* isn't the answer. It's all just too confusing—too emotionally draining, especially in the face of success.

a. Suicide:

Often, depression and withdrawal follows accomplishment and for a surprising number of males, status and public acclaim produce high levels of anxiety. Now—for a growing number—comes the hard part: what to do about it. For the lucky ones (the overwhelming minority) who have learned to cope with stress at a younger age, this problem is a non-issue. But worry about how to deal with status and public notoriety lead the vast majority of MTS to flawed decisions—ones they usually regret. Some even decide to commit suicide. There are innumerable stories of men who won the Lotto or suddenly came into large amounts of wealth and in the end couldn't deal with the pressure. Some turned to drink and drugs, some gave it all away, but some could only find peace and quiet by ending their life. Status and money didn't do much for them.

And then there's the other side of the coin. As Andy Warhol once said, "Everybody is famous for fifteen minutes," but the problem with that fiction is lately more and more of MTS believe they have a "right" to be famous for at least fifteen minutes, maybe longer. Fame or status becomes an end. So if they're not getting the recognition they think they deserve and they can't seem to identify with or get accepted by some group or sports team, depression and withdrawal sets in. Without significant societal support and safety-net systems in place to bridge the gap between expectations and reality, such members of MTS are left to deal with these issues on their own while society looks the other way and pretends nothing is wrong. Yet the facts show that male suicide is one of society's dirty little secrets.

At the beginning of the third millennium, MTS is choosing to end his life in record numbers. According to a report from Centers for Disease Control and Prevention, National Vital Statistics Report, Vol. 47, No.9, November 10, 1998, p.5, Table B in *Women Can't Hear What Men Don't Say* by Warren Farrell, Ph.D. (Tarcher Putnam (1999), males now commit suicide 4.5 times more often than women; adolescent and young adult males now commit suicide at four times the rate of girls and adolescent females, and it gets even worse as males arrive in their twenties (15-19 is 4:1; 20-24 is 6:1). Clearly, depression and withdrawal for men—young and old—should be a serious and high profile priority for all society, yet nobody but a few seems to even notice, and those who do often have an agenda.

In her book *Understanding Men's Passages: Discovering the New Map of Men's Lives* (Random House, 1998), Gail Sheehy falls into that trap. Because she wants her book to be age specific and have it mirror women's "passages," she ignores much of the facts currently available concerning male suicide.

Doctor Lionel Tiger, who is the Charles Darwin Professor of Anthropology at Rutgers University and the author of nine books, doesn't even mention suicide in his book *The Decline of Males* (Golden Books, 1999), despite the fact that he makes the following statement in his first chapter:

"This book is about an emerging pattern. Men and women may not discern it clearly, but the pattern underlies their experiences in industrial society. It is a pattern of growth in the confidence and power of women, and of the erosion in the confidence and power of men.

"What follows is a chronicle of the decline of men and the ascendancy of women. More women are having children without men, and therefore more men are without the love of families. Women as a group are working more and earning more. Men are working less and earning less. In 1998, for the first time in the United States, 'young women are completing high school and graduating from college at higher rates than their male peers,' which yields clear impact on the future of employment....These changes have also disenfranchised men from traditional social roles but have not offered men many new opportunities."

Apparently, Dr. Tiger didn't think suicide figured in this equation.

And Sam Keen doesn't mention suicide in his important book for males *Fire in the Belly: On Being A Man* (Bantam Books, 1991).

———

One prominent author who *does* include male suicide as a significant factor in the evolving social developments concerning MTS is Doctor Warren Farrell. On the dust-jacket to one of his four published books, he is described as: "The only man ever elected three times to the Board of the National Organization for Women (NOW)...Dr. Farrell's unique perspective comes not only from his background with NOW but also from being on the boards of three national men's organizations."

In addition to his 1999 book, Farrell also devotes an entire chapter to the controversial subject of male suicide in his book *The Myth of Male Power* (Simon & Schuster, 1993), in which he concludes with these words: "We need to hear when men communicate rather than deny they are communicating because they do it imperfectly, and then deny they suffer because they don't communicate. Until we do, men will not report their depression to therapists—or to anyone. They will be rough, tough cream puffs: the suicide class."

As we mentioned in Chapter One, the number of males committing suicide increases each year in alarming numbers, but we seldom hear about that. In *The Myth of Male Power*, Farrell asks, "If the Expression of Depression is Part of the Solution, Who is Helping Men Express Depression?" Immediately, he answers with these observations: "Are men taking responsibility to help themselves? Hardly. Men are still most likely to buy adventure books, financial journals, and sports magazines that teach men to solve problems, overcome barriers, or repress feelings. There are few men's shelters, 'masculist' psychologists, men's crisis lines, or men's centers. The biggest 'men's center' is San Quentin."

Prison. Now there's an example of self-destructive behavior we can all understand.

b. Incarceration:

Webster's Collegiate Dictionary defines "denial" (among other definitions) as: "a psychological defense mechanism in which confrontation with a personal problem or with reality is avoided by denying the existence of the problem or reality."

One of the biggest examples of denial and self-destructive behavior can be found in the nation's prisons and jails, especially since states and the federal government abandoned efforts to rehabilitate those in their care. ("By 1998, the United States had 1,500 prisons and 3,000 jails, the largest system in the world...By mid-1997, these institutions held an astonishing 1,725, 842 prisoners, a huge number of them drug offenders," *The Dark Side of Man.*) Prisoners are no longer challenged by professional counselors as to their behavior—either in or out of prison. Instead, "cons" are warehoused from society until they've done enough time to warrant a parole hearing (95% of all prisoners in the U.S. are male). After that, if prisoners "act" sufficiently contrite, and say the right things to impress their parole board, they're allowed back on the streets where the recidivism rates run 80% or higher. (According to *The Dark Side of Man*, "on average, 14 people are murdered, 48 women are raped, and 578 people are robbed each day—*all by convicted criminals returned to the streets on probation or early parole.*")

In other words, without professional assistance, prisoners find old bad habits hard or impossible to break. But that's not news; men and women under the direct care of a professional counselor have a recidivism rate in excess of 50%. Ask anyone in an AA or NA program; participants who experience a "relapse" are commonplace. The difference is those in AA or NA understand that—like the horseback rider thrown from the horse—they are well-advised to immediately recommence their long journey back to "clean and sober" living. Parolees or prisoners are under no such limitations. Just as long as they "keep their nose clean," the criminal justice system will leave them alone.

The principle difference between someone who regularly utilizes professional counseling and a prisoner who does not is their view of the world: The former must confront the reality of their behavior on a daily, weekly, or bi-weekly basis. Prisoners do not, so they're free to blame someone else. There's no one in authority except their warden or parole officer to remind and emphasize that they're in charge of their own behavior. Most "ex-cons" have little or no use for authority—an attitude that usually goes back to their childhood. The facts are the devil or their pastor or their father or mother or social worker or teacher did *not* make them commit their crime(s). Most prisoners made a choice way back when they first began breaking the law, and they've continued making a majority of wrong choices ever since (of course there are exceptions).

The average prisoner does not accept the fact of their own responsibility, and that's why such an attitude is called denial. And continuing to make choices which result in him/her going back to prison is further proof of a life-style of self-destruction. Because so many more males than women populate our U.S. correctional facilities (approximately 20 to 1), such self-destructive behavior is—in the main—a major problem for MTS but one the white, middle-class segments of society currently believe can be cured by "getting tough on crime." They've somehow come to the myopic conclusion that criminal behavior is like an infectious virus which can be cured by vaccinations such as "zero tolerance, three-strike," or "death-penalty" laws. They read the public relations rhetoric pumped out by the FBI or the local police agencies about the various "reductions in violent crime," then climb into bed each night convinced that all's right with the world and God's in His heaven—more societal denial.

The simple truth is that due to the reduction of police officers relative to the growing population in the suburbs, many "small" violent crimes go unreported, especially crimes against property—auto break-ins, shop-lifting, petty larceny, pick-pocketing, etc. Most people would rather just call their insurance company to see if they're covered. If not, they'd just as soon forget the whole thing, and not have to wait forever for the police to show up and fill out a long, mindless report they know the police are too undermanned to investigate, and run the risk for having the authorities stomping around in their private lives. The dirty little secret is that the public—especially the lower class, the poor, the immigrants, and the disenfranchised—has lost confidence in the police and the criminal justice system in general.

Once again, Michael Ghiglieri writes on-point concerning this dark side of society: "It is no surprise, then, that only 19 percent of Americans in 1996 expressed great confidence in the criminal justice system."

The only justice (in the minds of average and poor Americans) is for those who can afford expensive lawyers or can convince "politically correct" *pro-bono* organizations (those who "selectively" aid the poor only after deciding that a particular case will help them raise money from the white, middle and upper class "donor-types") of the validity of the wrongs done to them. For most families, the bureaucracy and the law-enforcement agencies of this country cannot be trusted. For most children and their families, this disillusionment begins in grammar school—a place marketed to the public as being "family-friendly." But that's really not the case if you're a child of color or poverty or a single-parent family or immigrant parents or non-English-speaking parents.

It's doubly deadly if you're a adolescent male.

c. The Public School Holocaust:

Holocaust? "Surely you exaggerate," you're thinking as you read the above sub-headline. None of the known governments—as we begin the Third Millennium—of Western Civilization conducts itself in any manner which closely resembles the Holocaust of Nazi-held Europe before and during WW II. You're right, there are NOT trains jam-packed with unsuspecting families headed for so-called "re-location centers." And city police forces are NOT dragging families out of their homes in the middle of the night to fill those trains (except if you're thought to be peddling large amounts of drugs, or if one of the federal or state taxing agencies decides you owe them money).

That said, there actually is a major Holocaust taking place right under our very noses in major cities and towns throughout the Unites States. Police don't compel the victims to participate, legislatures do. Victims aren't packed on trains, instead they ride yellow buses to where millions are systematically poisoned and maimed for life.

Here's how it works. Based on so-called annual "reading" tests, urban students are arbitrarily assigned a "ranking" in their respective school district. Those the most "below grade" are arbitrarily assigned to remedial reading classes—parents have little say in the matter and are often not even informed until after the fact. In the main, these classes are manned by teachers and aides who have no credentials on how to teach reading or special education. Such classes typically last two-four hours each school day and are usually simply a "warehousing" exercise. When the children (usually young males) get hostile or fidgety during such classes, they're labeled a "discipline problem." They're written up, their parents called in for a conference (often in a language they don't understand) and put on notice that the behavior must improve, otherwise their child will be suspended or dismissed from that school.

Now begins a predictable process of the student changing schools or indulging in truancy behavior or both. Once truancy enters the case, the student is assigned to the juvenile court system and after that, it's usually a one-way ticket to drugs, gangs, breaking the law, and eventual incarceration in an adult facility—in other words, another lost life, another statistic; a living breathing person who is walking around, but for all practical purposes is dead and just doesn't know it. These unfortunate young men (in the main) are the human male equivalent of a chicken running around with its head cut off.

Federal law stipulates that school systems who receive certain kinds of federal and state funding are supposed to seek out children who are having trouble with their reading and/or writing skills based on state academic content standards. Schools are mandated to intervene and bring to bear all the services and professional expertise necessary to help these students, regardless of race, religion, or national origin. But too often they do not. Those who generally get the most benefit from these kinds of funding programs are from white, middle-class neighborhoods—those who need it least.

And guess which students are usually found in these lowest "rankings"? The poor, those whose parents cannot speak English, those with learning disabilities, those who have been incorrectly taught to read, and those who live in ghetto neighborhoods, especially single-parent families. In other words, those least able to defend themselves, those least knowledgeable about how the system works and what their legal rights are, those most generally fearful of bureaucracy. In other words, the weak, the poor, and the disenfranchised.

Why does this happen with such regularity? It's all about who gets up off the couch and goes to the polls on election day. Those who vote get the attention of politicians which then translates itself into resources. Those who don't vote get only conversation and promises, not resources. Lack of resources translates into insufficient teachers and staff with insufficient training and assets.

Bottom line? A Holocaust is currently under way in the United States—one that is being inflicted on our children by the public school system. According to experts in the field, between ten and twenty-five percent of all students are basically being written off by taxpayer-funded schools. And of that group, the vast majority of the students written off are adolescent males from: ghetto households; families where English is seldom spoken at home; single-parent (usually women) homes; illegal immigrant homes where the families live in constant fear of any governmental authority.

The problem is we can't see this crime being committed; it's virtually invisible unless we can spare the time for long hours in the classroom to fully grasp the truth of the intellectual abuse taking place there. And when the adolescent male's report card comes out, he usually has a truthful explanation for why he did poorly, but most adults ignore it. "Kids from that part of town are just liars anyway, right?"

Most often—according to the teachers and principals—Johnny's grades are down because he didn't do his homework. "But he's a good boy," or a "smart boy" his parent(s) will say, "so why isn't he doing his homework?" Good question. What's bothering Johnny now spirals into a higher state of anxiety because the public school system seldom takes the trouble to unearth the real answer for these kids from "the wrong side of the tracks." It's much easier to blame the boy's parent(s) or his friends or his history and behavior. If he were a dolphin, bird, or chimpanzee, society would greet a similar report card problem with an attitude of loving care and benevolent curiosity. But since he's only a young member of MTS and a minority, "we need to show him right away that we're not going to put up with any more of his crap. He needs to know who's boss!"

In their book *Raising Cain: Protecting The Emotional Life Of Boys*, Dan Kindlon and Michael Thompson—two of America's leading child psychologists—make the following points: "Studies that track children's development through the school years suggest that, by the third grade, a child has established a pattern of learning that shapes the course of his or her entire school career. We see this clearly with boys: the first two years in school are a critical moment of entry into that world of learning, but boys' relative immaturity and the lack of fit they so often experience in school set them up to fail. Many boys who are turned off to school at a young age never re-find the motivation to become successful learners. Even among those who press on to achieve success later in life, the emotional scars of those troubled years do not fade."

The visible manifestation of this public school disgrace takes place on a daily basis in the juvenile court system of our cities and towns. Each weekday morning and sometimes on weekends, millions of families (usually of color) across the country—fathers, mothers, children, uncles, aunts, and grandparents—line up and wait their turn for the government to announce how badly one or all of them has failed. It's always the family's fault—the accused boy, the parents, the grandparents, or a combination of all three.

The school system which has primary responsibility for him 6-12 hours of every weekday is never brought to task. How well they empower him and tap into his abilities and enthusiasm is never questioned. How badly they misdiagnose his educational needs is never quantified. How much educational malpractice they perform on him is never discussed or addressed. How much intellectual and emotional abuse they heap on him day-after-day is never considered by the courts, even though these public educational institutions have custody and control of the child between 38 and 75 percent of his waking weekday hours. The school systems are never held "accountable"—individual teachers (and their unions) or principals are by the politicians, but never the curricula dictated by the state or local school board. The lack of special education resources mandated by federal legislation and often ignored by the local school superintendent is never brought to a public accounting.

Worse yet, because of the lack of sufficient funding for the juvenile courts, there's a huge backlog of cases. Sometimes it takes months or years for final disposition of an individual referral from a school truancy report. The child can sometimes be separated from his family at the court's direction for a significant proportion of this time period—thus exacerbating an already traumatic experience.

For most families, it's a lose-lose situation and a possible foreshadowing of future events. In his book *Lost Boys*, Doctor James Garbarino makes this observation: "I believe that the social environment across most of the country has become less welcoming to highly vulnerable children, that is, those who live under difficult social and emotional conditions and therefore soak up social poisons." Boys from poor neighborhoods, single-parent families, or families whose members do not speak English at home would clearly qualify as "vulnerable children."

Adult prison statistics would seem to bear out the "vulnerable child" paradigm. In a footnote for his book *The Myth of Male Power*, Doctor Warren Farrell writes: "According to *Young Black Men in the Criminal Justice System* by Marc Mauer (Washington, D.C.: The Sentencing Project, 1990), 436,000 black males of all ages are in college; 609,690 young black men (50 percent more) are under the control of the criminal justice system. (White males, on the other hand, are more than four times as likely to be in college as in the criminal justice system.)"

Still, despite the injustice of it all, most observers agree that in the final analysis, each member of MTS must take responsibility for his own deeds and consequences. "Life's not fair," is the well-known mantra of this kind of thinking. But for the emotionally ill-equipped male (read the vast majority of MTS), it's of little comfort to hear such left-brained pseudo-psychology. "No one seems to care; no one seems to understand my problems," he says to himself. "It's like talking to a wall."

d. Drugs & Alcohol:

Since institutional religion or "the man" (read other establishment institutions historically used by civilized humankind as a resource during times of turmoil and anguish) offer no real answers for those members of MTS who feel lost, and neither does television, the movies, the whole music scene, the theater, the Internet, nor (apparently) books, that leaves few choices—or so goes the conventional wisdom. A local journalist overheard a "boomer" who was well into his cups and talking to a bartender about the whole problem of what role males should play in modern society. "It's really a drag, man. Everybody is just a freakin' liar…nobody knows what's really goin' on. Think I'll just get high. I mean like totally wasted!"

Such has been the thought process (or lack thereof) for an overwhelming majority of MTS during the past 30-40 years. They can't discern insightful answers and don't know where to turn, so they just drop out. MTS has lost himself. The outward signs of this malaise are the anger of the males in the inner cities; the use and abuse of various foreign substances; and all kinds of mind-numbing activities—whether they be 24-hours of TV, 10 hours of football watching, daily boozing and gambling, or the eternal pursuit of women. Individually or collectively, these activities mean a male has found a medium of denial where he can survive without a serious "confrontation with a personal problem or with reality…by denying the existence of the problem or reality." It also means that the male will once again postpone achieving the natural joy and happiness that could be nurturing both to his own life and those he loves.

MTS has now become a life-form in search of an identity with a new and changing world where his identity can be challenged as quickly as the weather can change in Kansas. It's a mammoth undertaking made all the more difficult by MTS' and society's general unwillingness to agree that a problem actually exists (read denial). Some males see the issues with insight and understanding, but many of them think society's so-called problems with MTS are lot of feminist male-baiting.

One school of thought was recently advanced in *The New York Times Magazine* in an article entitled "The HE Hormone." In his piece, writer Andrew Sullivan analyzes the possibility that many of the problems associated with anti-social male behavior these days can be explained by testosterone. At one point, he observed, "But fears of natural difference still haunt the debate about equality. Many feminists have made tenacious arguments about the lack of any substantive physical or mental differences between men and women as if political equality of the sexes depended on it. But to rest the equality of women on the physical and psychological equivalence of the sexes is to rest it on sand."

Women too have trouble agreeing about what the problem is; they generally acknowledge there's a problem, but after that, opinions widely vary. While the various forms of the "blame game" and denial continue, the United States and the rest of Western Civilization have developed a monumental plague called substance abuse. It permeates all aspects of society—from the highest levels of government to the upper and middle class bedrooms and boardrooms to the ghetto streets and elementary school classrooms.

"More boys than girls are involved in crime, alcohol, and drugs," writes Christina Hoff Summers in her book *The War Against Boys: How Misguided Feminism Is Harming Our Young Men* (Simon & Schuster, 2000). She cites several sources including the U.S. Department of Education, *The Condition of Education* (Washington, D.C.: U.S. Department of Education, 1997).

Doctor Garbarino in *Lost Boys* is even more forthcoming: "Hard drugs have spread throughout the United States; virtually every community in the country has a drug subculture. For 1997 the Centers for Disease Control and Prevention reported, in the annual *Youth Risk Behavior Surveillance*, that 9 percent of all high-school-age males had used cocaine. Moreover, 50 percent of adolescent boys reported having used marijuana, and 30 percent had used it in the previous month. After a decline in overall drug use among teenagers, which started in 1976 (when 45 percent admitted to some drug use) and continued to 1994, the reported overall use is on the increase again and now stands at 36 percent. What is more, heavy alcohol use among teenage boys is common: 37 percent of the boys reported that they drank five or more drinks on one occasion at least once in the previous month."

Doctors Kindlon and Thompson continue the sad saga of denial and substance abuse: "In high school yearbooks where students are allowed to include their favorite photos of good times, it is not unusual to see this classic picture: a gregarious group of six or eight boys, smiling broadly with their arms around one another's shoulders. They are, of course, drunk, maybe stoned as well. In the adolescent boy culture, boys use alcohol and drugs as the basis for a good time and to break down some of the emotional barriers they've built. But even though emotions may come to the surface while drinking, this is a manly activity, so the absence of stoicism can be excused. You are not culpable: almost any action performed while drunk can be dismissed the next day, so it is safe and allows them to feel close to someone for a little while. It temporarily dulls the pain of isolation and loneliness.

"Alcohol is an analgesic—a killer of all kinds of pain—through its effects on the brain's endogenous opiate system, responsible for producing that morphine-like substance that relieves our pain."

And after the follies of his painful youth, MTS must then face the choice of what to do as a responsible adult. Doctor Lionel Tiger brings us the last chapter of this poignant search for answers in his book *The Decline of Males*: "While countless women take drugs, illegal drug users are overwhelmingly male. The fantasies of omnipotence and invulnerability, and the reality of escape, that men purchase when they buy drugs have generated industries which have enriched and corrupted whole countries and caused radical convulsions in the flows of cash and wealth in the world."

9. Brief Summary of Chapter Three:

In this chapter, we have examined many of the impediments facing MTS in his attempt to rediscover in modern society a meaningful role for himself, his sons, grandsons, and succeeding generations. We have charted two major turning points in this never-ending journey for all of society and especially the male species: the Industrial Revolution and the Mass Communications Revolution.

Through all of history, the role of the female has remained and will continue to remain fairly static at its most basic biological level because of her child-bearing abilities. Because of that basic fact, it is the male that must do most of the adapting to the changing environments brought by history. We've observed how MTS has used the confusion about his role as a catalyst to enslave or subjugate the female—wars, rape, invented fears about women's occult powers, second-class citizenship for females; the list is as endless as the male imagination.

Yet even in face of the overwhelming evidence at hand as we begin the Third Millennium, MTS is still heavily into denial. And we have explored many of the current examples of the male (as well as much of the rest of society) trying to pretend that little of any importance has changed since the dawn of the Industrial or Mass Communications Revolutions. The pitiable end-result of this sophisticated but brutal denial comprises the basis for so much of what is wrong with 21st Century Humankind. But before I can recommend in good conscience those avenues I believe offer the best hope of curing these problems, we must first discuss that which cannot be predicted: *The Variables*.

Chapter Four

Variables Along The Way To Newness

In the last part of the 20th century, best-selling author Michael Crichton elevated Chaos Theory from the private realm of scientists and mathematicians to the public consciousness. Through his two novels (*Jurassic Park* and *The Lost World*) about DNA, dinosaurs, extinction of species, and "the rise and decline of earth's species in a four-million-year life cycle," he placed the question of the future of mankind front and center. One of his characters—a mathematician and scientist—explains Chaos Theory to a curious audience with surprising clarity (especially for our purposes): "[W]e do not recognize how continuously active our planet is. Just in the last fifty thousand years— a geological blink of an eye—the rain forests have severely contracted, then expanded again. Rain forests aren't an ageless feature of the planet; they're actually rather new. As recently as 10,000 years ago, when there were human hunters on the American continent, an ice pack extended as far down as New York City . . .

"What I wish to propose is that complex animals become extinct not because of a change in their physical adaptation to their environment, but because of their behavior. I would suggest that the latest thinking in chaos theory, or nonlinear dynamics, provides tantalizing hints of how this happens.

"It suggests to us that behavior of complex animals can change very rapidly, and not always for the better. It suggests that behavior can cease to be responsive to the environment, and lead to decline and death. It suggests that animals may stop adapting. Is this what happened to the dinosaurs? Is this the true cause of their disappearance? We may never know. But it is no accident that human beings are so interested in dinosaur extinction. The decline of the dinosaurs allowed mammals—including us—to flourish. And that leads us to wonder whether the disappearance of the dinosaurs is going to be repeated, sooner or later, by us as well. Whether at the deepest level the fault lies not in blind fate—in some fiery meteor from the skies—but in our own behavior. At the moment we have no answer."

The variables at work in suggesting that MTS might adopt new ways of thinking in order to avoid the fate of the dinosaur has many aspects.

A. *The Chaos Theory and Its Relevance:*

In Crichton's *The Lost World,* the same character who spoke above gives another talk entitled, "Life at the Edge of Chaos" in which he advances his analysis of chaos theory "as it applie[s] to evolution." He stands before a knowledgeable audience of scientists "interested in the implications of chaos theory." The author's narrator goes on to point out that, "What they had in common was a belief that the complexity of the world concealed an underlying order which had previously eluded science, and which would be revealed by chaos theory, now known as complexity theory. In the words of one, complexity theory was 'the science of the twenty-first century.'"

The narrator is also quick to point out that these various theories have only been made possible in large part by the computer. Nevertheless, the research is new and the findings surprising. "It did not take long before the scientists began to notice [in response to the aforementioned fictional speech] that complex systems showed certain common behaviors. They realized that these behaviors could not be explained by analyzing the components of the systems. The time-honored scientific approach of reductionism—taking the watch apart to see how it worked—didn't get you anywhere with complex systems, because the interesting behavior seemed to rise from the spontaneous interaction of the components. The behavior wasn't planned or directed; it just happened. Such behavior was therefore called 'self-organizing'.... Complex systems tend to locate themselves at a place we call 'the edge of chaos.' We imagine the edge of chaos as a place where there is enough innovation to keep a living system vibrant, and enough stability to keep it from collapsing into anarchy. It is a zone of conflict and upheaval, where the old and the new are constantly at war. Finding the balance point must be a delicate matter—if a living system drifts too close, it risks falling over into incoherence and dissolution; but if the system moves too far away from the edge, it becomes rigid, frozen, destructive, totalitarian. Both conditions lead to extinction. Too much change is as destructive as too little. Only at the edge of chaos can complex systems flourish."

Homo sapiens as a species certainly qualifies as a "complex system." The big unanswered questions are: Have we moved too far away from the edge and are we about to become "rigid, frozen, and destructive; or, are we too close to the edge and about to fall "into incoherence and dissolution"?

Before the Renaissance, one could have made a convincing case for mankind having moved too far from the edge, but since Medieval times we've abruptly reversed field and headed in the opposite direction. When we especially look back over the past 150 years, our flight into anarchy appears virtually unchecked, with all recent attempts to brake this inclination to inflict self-destruction going virtually unheeded. Mankind seems determined to drive itself into extinction, no matter what anyone else says.

A second aspect of Chaos Theory is its cyclical characteristics. Simply stated this theory holds that in the fullness of time, all activities in a cyclical system return to their original point. In their textbook called *Turbulent Mirror: An Illustrated Guide to Chaos Theory and the Science of Wholeness* by John Briggs and F. David Peat (Harper & Row, 1989), the authors refer to such systems as "Systems That Come Back to Their Cages." They also refer to them as "limit cycles," i.e., "An important instance of a limit cycle is the predator-prey system....Scientists noticed on the yellowing pages of the Hudson Bay ledgers that over decades good and bad seasons for lynx and snowshoe hare pelts had followed a cyclical pattern which suggested that the population of these animals oscillated in a definite cycle."

However, limit cycles can have more than one period or cycle within them, and they're called coupled oscillating or periodic behavior. "A system that looks almost periodic but never exactly repeats itself is called, quite logically, quasi-periodic." Also after long testing, scientists discovered that, "At this point we notice that the kind of nature described so far by attractors is quite regular....It is a classical world where scientists can predict the behavior of even quite complicated systems for long periods ahead. Scientists have even developed the notion of 'asymptotic predictability'—meaning that even if they are ignorant about the exact position of a system at the moment, they are confident that no matter how far into the future they look, it will be moving somewhere on the surface of a torus (a two-dimensional phase cycle) and not wandering around randomly in phase space."

In other words, Chaos Theory does allow for the possibility of humankind to return to a former method of operation for civilization—one where the male was not so dominant, so uncooperative towards the female, so patriarchal. That does not mean that Chaos Theory predicts such a return; it merely provides that theatrically it could happen—it allows for the very real possibility of such an event. Let us remember that up until 5,000 years ago—approximately the same time that the alphabet came into wide usage—men and women operated at an almost equal basis in society—as co-operators of society, if you will. Women were not chattel then, nor were they second-class citizens. Also Goddesses were as much a part of those civilizations as were male Gods—in some cases Goddesses, especially Mother Goddess, were much more powerful than the Gods.

Despite such interesting speculation, there can be no ignoring the significant variant role technology will play in the future of MTS and all humankind for that matter, 'asymptotic predictability' or not.

B. Technology & Its Run-Away Consequences:

In as much as humankind is currently experiencing a Mass Communications Revolution the likes of which we have never witnessed before, it does not take much imagination to foresee the incredible possibilities for the near and distant future. By the middle of this century, instant combined communications of every sort will be routine for any inhabitant of this planet who may wish it. Virtual intelligence will be commonplace; any command we utter to a computer will be executed immediately, including typing all our letters and articles and stories, folding, and mailing them for us. Whatever so-called cutting-edge computer technology is in place by the end of this year will become obsolete 30 days into the new year. The pace of new technology in all fields is breath-taking and will remain so far beyond anything we can now possibly envision. In 5-10 years we will look back at the body of knowledge of today and laugh at how crude it was—that's how rapid and sophisticated the new technology is going to be—in all fields.

Among the leaders of this rapid outbreak of scientific and technical advancement will be Biology, Medicine, Astronomy, Outer Space Travel, Genetic Engineering, and Weather Control. In the field of Physics, there's recent news that one of the staples of scientific knowledge is even under a cloud of suspicion—the speed of light. As we go to press, media accounts claim that a new medium faster than the speed of light has been uncovered. Moreover, apparently anti-matter exists and also contains the potential for some kind of movement of objects and/or people swifter than the speed of light—a mind-boggling thought. So does that mean that Einstein's Theory of Relativity is wrong or is it merely incomplete as we came to understand it? Pretty heady stuff!

And on the dark side, there are the possibilities for future large-scale bloodshed—international terrorism, rogue nuclear theft and attack, biological attacks on public transportation like those unleashed in European and Eastern subways, or poison gas assaults on large buildings or enclosed shopping malls. There's no predicting such events—Lord knows that deranged men and women the world over are planning similar episodes as you read this page. Our best hopes for frustrating their plans lie with new technology and its ability to stay one step ahead of these demented men and women.

One of the consequences of this explosion of technological innovation will also be an increasing assault on institutions—government, morals, religion, family, law and order, life and death itself. Virtually everything will be called into question; it will be as the Peter O'Toole character said in *Lawrence of Arabia* after being told "It is written" that a man who had fallen off his camel during the night would perish in the blazing desert. "Nothing is written," he snarled at Omar Sharif after returning from those shifting sands with the fallen man alive and well on the back of his camel. "Nothing!"

Humankind is on the verge of declaring itself a God unto itself. Nietzsche still lives in the minds and hearts of too many men and women. Is there any hope?

C. The Role of the "New" Religions:

In truth, attacks on the establishment have already begun. Institutional religion was the first to feel the full brunt of the "boomer" disillusionment. People still need something to believe in—something bigger than themselves—so "New Age" thinkers have brought us "pure energy" in lieu of God; the power of God has been replaced by "the force." Where the most important thing about life used to be leading a good or righteous life or to go to heaven after we die, now (according to the New Agers) a sign of leading meaningful life is to be in "balance." Nevertheless, these initial forays into religious substitution could seem pale by comparison to what lies around the corner once the technological explosion jumps into high gear in the next few years.

The "New Age" and "alternate" religious movement has so far been rather tame in its attempt to supplant the "old" religions, but the newer religious movements might not be as benign. Like Socialism and Communism and Atheism before them, the so-called "Newest Age" faiths could see these institutional dinosaurs as the enemy. High on their list might be a number of the unresolved issues of current Western Civilization theology; things like: Divorce, Pre-Martial Sex, Contraceptive Sex, What Is The Purpose of Marriage, Child Custody and Visitation Rights, Homosexuality, Masturbation, Abortion, What Constitutes a Family, The Role of Women in Religion, and Why Are There No Goddesses?

Whether or not all the above topics get addressed and resolved by the steadily growing "alternate religious" movement, one of the things that must be resolved—sooner rather than later for there to be order in society—will be the dual questions of personal responsibility and the value of life, all life. Those two issues, more than many others, have been forced to the forefront of societal consciousness by the technological explosion currently stampeding through Western Civilization. Yet, humankind seems more reluctant than ever to confront these delicate subjects. There are no easy answers, and humankind has not had enough time to really consider all the ramifications in light of the newest information, so there seems to be this unspoken conspiracy (except for a small minority) among the politicians, journalists, and academics to avoid speaking directly to these topics. In other words, we're into denial there as well.

And speaking of denial, the question of how those who agree with me can "comfortably" lead western humankind into a reevaluation of its 5,000 year-old-habit of having only one God—and a male one at that—is probably the issue that will capture the most attention by readers; it also holds the potential to become the most volatile variable in this whole sub-section. It's difficult to predict which gender will resist a change in this concept with the greatest tenacity. It certainly would not be in keeping with past performances of MTS for him to lead the way into this progressive-approach construct concerning religion.

It would be like expecting blacksmiths at the end of the 19th century to lead the way in welcoming the new form of transportation—the automobile—despite the fact that it would put the blacksmiths virtually out of business. Of course, enlightened blacksmiths did that very thing and immediately found themselves in the automobile repair business and as much or more in demand than they had ever been before with new customers (in general) who had more disposable income and didn't mind paying top dollar for his services. But then, nobody has recently accused MTS of working in his own best interests *and* those of society in general, have they? The truth is that once upon a time MTS did just that—but not lately. And that's part of the problem. Around 150 years ago, MTS got away from the habit of doing the right thing just because it was the right thing. Robert Bly was right: Western society hasn't been the same since.

Chapter Five

Summary & Suggestions

A. Overview & Summary:

The following is a brief look backwards at what we've covered and why.

1. **Chapter One—Where Are We?:** Contains incidents and statistics which emphasize the deteriorating situation in modern civilization regarding the male and a brief overview of the development of humankind from its earliest forms to now and how it has managed to survive 3,500,000 years.

2. **Chapter Two—How did We Get Here?** Given the mess western society is in as we begin the Third Millennium, how did we get there?
   a. **A Review of Pre-Historic Society** and how it developed from its earliest pre-historic times—600,000 BC—up until the introduction of farming around 10,000 to 6,000 BC.

b. **A Brief History of Goddess in Herder/Farmer Times** and what roles Goddesses played in those societies; what roles the male played.

c. **Why the Demise of the Goddess?** traces the history of Goddesses beginning with the discovery of the alphabet, the beginning of written history, and the male's subjugation of the female. We then follow recorded history through these three essential aspects of the disappearance of the Goddess—most always coinciding with the male's inhumanity to the female.

1. **Chapter Three—The Main Problems For MTS** in trying to understand the challenges facing him.

   a. **The Industrial Revolution—1850:Patriarchy's Last Gasp** explains how this important moment in history marked the last high-water mark (such as it was) when the male really had any accurate notion of what being a man meant—what his role then was in terms of society's attitudes toward him.

   b. **Forgetting How to Be a Man: The Beginning of The End** is dominated by the interview and discussion between Bill Moyers and Robert Bly about how it came to pass that the post Industrial Revolution male lost his compass with respect to what is expected of him by the rest of society and himself; there's an emphasis on the role fathers play in this complicated dynamic.

   c. **Denial & Its Many Forms** lists eight major categories of behavior in modern society each of which, in and of themselves, makes a strong case for the western male's predisposition to denial and avoidance of a confrontation with the real problems he faces today.

   d. **Summary** briefly reviews the subjects covered in this chapter.

1. **Variables Along the Way To Newness** discusses some of the many factors to consider before suggesting that MTS should adopt new ways of thinking in order to avoid the fate of the dinosaur.
   a. **Chaos Theory** explores two variable aspects of this theory which have application for the male and his behavior relative to history.

   b. **Technology & Its Run-Away Consequences** addresses the variable possibilities which no one can predict with the advent of such rapid technological development in so many different fields of human knowledge.

   c. **The Role of the "New" Religions** suggests a few of the potential religious scenarios which might develop as a result of the rapid growth of technological hardware and information. The old institutions are probably out of business or obsolete, and the new ones will seem like nothing we've seen before.

B. Suggestions For the Future of MTS:

As I said in the Introduction, I consider this a health care volume, a societal health care book. The issue under discussion here is the future role of the male (MTS) in Western Civilization. We've focused our attention so far on what *has been*—the good, the negative, and the unacceptable—for the past 5,000 years or so; mostly it's a tale of the male's inhumanity to the female and himself—especially since 1850.

The main question yet to be resolved is a clear sense of purpose—where do we go from here, long-term? What behaviors MTS and the rest of society decide to pursue in this regard during the next few years or even the next decade is not so much my concern. My hope for this book is to provide a framework within which all society—and MTS in particular—can formulate a more nurturing, long-range role for MTS than the crumbling, obsolete, and virtually extinct model he's been blindly pursuing for the past five millennia.

The problem is we're talking about change, but the virus of change has to be understood and harnessed for our collective betterment. In a progress-oriented society, there comes a point where we don't understand if progress benefits humankind or is simply out of control and on its way to be becoming a force for further destruction. Within such a construct, the thrust of technology and its attempt to create more goods and services bumps up against the quality of life and the over-utilization of the Earth's capacity to provide. Currently, humankind is experiencing such an era, and the result is a qualitative thinning of our lives. Our reality is being stolen by the narcotic of mass communications. Society has invaded that which was once natural and innate to humankind with a mind-numbing narcotic and a need to hype product. When Seed-desire (the most basic drive within MTS) and Earth-desire (the most basic drive within WTS) are gone and there's no more ability or inclination to nourish—life worth living is at an end. No love, just aggression and product.

Society in general—and MTS in particular—needs to return to nurturement as the focus of what we do. We've observed how humankind has distanced itself from nature because it learned to think and use the alphabet—thus providing license for that disconnect. As a result, humankind now finds itself closer and closer to becoming an interchangeable part in the engine of technology—one of our new religions (although most males would deny that as well). College and graduate students don't pursue Liberal Arts studies anymore. "That would be a waste," they parrot like new hideous offspring of *The Stepford Wives*. Our children don't build tree houses or play hide-and-seek in the woods any more, they watch MTV or get on an Internet chat room or play video war games. And the adults are no better: Growing numbers of men and women now get happily paid to spend whole weeks—day and night—indoors, glued to a monitor and keyboard. If they leave the house, they must bring their laptop and cellphone. When they're in church or at the opera, the cleric or stage manager now finds it necessary remind such people to turn off their machinery, or, at the very least, mute the ringing device.

Humankind belongs in nature—it's our roots, our basic habitat. It's where the love is, and, instinctively, we know it. It brings us relaxation, order, and sense of connection with our ancestors going back hundreds of thousands of years. In that sense we are like a plant, and violent change would be the same as taking a plant that grows in the desert and replanting it in Alaska. If we change our environment abruptly, like plants, we will whither and die.

So for MTS, I have chosen another nature-based metaphor—that of the caterpillar who instinctive knows when it is time to go into the cocoon. MTS instinctively knows he can be something more beautiful—like say, a butterfly. The cocoon knows he must come out as something more attractive, more interesting, and more colorful because this world no longer needs the old useless caterpillar—the male role paradigm of the past 5,000 years. Instinctively, all members of MTS know something is drastically wrong with what modern society has carved out and labeled "manhood." MTS knows he can be more, much more.

Historically when a male's problems became too overwhelming to consider in the normal course of human events, he made a retreat into seclusion and contemplation (witness the behavior of Jesus Christ, Lawrence of Arabia, Patton, and Jimmy Carter). No reason to change that tradition; MTS is going to have to go on a series of massive group retreats and invest considerable blocks of time to rethinking the whole situation—where he's been, where he is, where he'd like to be. Of particular concern should be his current obsession with self-destructive behavior. As long as society in general allows this "denial" to continue unchallenged, we all suffer, especially women and children. And in case any members of MTS who are reading this book haven't figured it out by now, the whole reason for the so-called feminist movement was because we (members of MTS) basically abandoned the women and children when we went off to the cities in response to the Industrial Revolution. We forgot about our families and their needs. We were too busy being angry or afraid at the way things had changed.

Our new model should be one of co-operation with our co-partners in society. In every respect and where practical, males and females should be co-equal in terms of duties, responsibilities, rewards, and consequences. Obviously, as a general rule, males bearing children or females playing men's professional football won't work, but those are the exceptions. Our goal should be one of inclusion first, and exclusion only when we have solid experience that clearly makes such inclusion impractical or destructive.

To this point, what I am suggesting is not new. Many have already written—and far more eloquently—about the need for the above-mentioned changes in what males do. But what I'm proposing is far more complex and demanding. It goes to the very essence of what the male's role should be in modern western society—not just for the next few decades, but far into the future. And the changes I'm suggesting could be as cataclysmic in its impact upon the history of *Homo Sapiens* as was the male's decision to abandon his hunter-gatherer lifestyle in favor of herder-farmer ways some 15,000 to 10,000 years ago.

C. A New Way of Thinking and Doing:

So the issue for MTS now becomes, What specifically should a man do? How should a real man comport himself in his day-to-day living? What are manly traits—traits which will have application and relevance for the next several millennia and which all of society, especially the female, will recognize and accept as real, desirable, and necessary? It seems obvious that society needs a new paradigm—the one we've been using for the past 5,000 years no longer has relevance. It is an old construct which has run through the Chaos Theory cycle and is returning to "its cage."

ONE: MTS and the rest of society must begin with the notion that in order to agree on a new and acceptable model of behavior for a real "man", humankind—as a species—must see and acknowledge the seriousness of problem. The empirical evidence can no longer be ignored: The current model, in light of the realities of the present state of human affairs in western culture, does not work. Each of us—men, women, and children—need to abandon our predisposition to the narcotic of denial in favor of getting on with the business of finding a honest and winning solution which benefits all.

TWO: Humankind needs to "break out of the box" of conventional thinking. In their book *The Ending of Time*, authors Dr. J. Krishnamurti and Dr. David Bohm challenge much of our assumptions about the fundamental issues of existence. They begin with the question, "Has humanity taken a wrong turn, which has brought about endless division, conflict, and destruction?" They conclude that the answer is in the affirmative, then spend the majority of the book discussing each of the major components of this "wrong turn."

To summarize their evocative book, the publisher (HarperSanFrancisco) writes on the back cover: "[B]ut this is not something from which there is no escape. There is an insistence that humankind can change fundamentally; but this requires going from one's narrow and particular interests toward a general, and ultimately moving still deeper into that purity of compassion, love, and intelligence that originates in the ground beyond thought, beyond time, even beyond emptiness. This means giving one's mind, one's heart, one's whole being, to the inquiry carried on throughout these discussions."

That is why I have suggested the metaphor of the caterpillar, the cocoon, and the butterfly. All humankind—especially MTS—needs to give this entire problem serious thought through meaningful dialogue, writings, quiet contemplation and meditation. No one said it was going to be easy or that it could be accomplished quickly.

THREE: I've come to believe Robert Bly had it right. Once humankind reaches a consensus about the paradigm for what it means to be "a man," society needs to go back to the tradition of male mentors or "Male Mothers," as Bly refers to them. As you may remember, these are males who know what it means to be a real man, (under the old paradigm: a happy combination of warrior, nurturer, and someone who is unafraid to act) who makes it his business to pass this knowledge onto succeeding generations by committing time and patience to such an endeavor. In Bly's view, these males would see it as part of their responsibilities as males or MTS—their contribution to a healthy and nurturing society.

FOUR: There needs to be a return to the concept of what the Romans used to call *res publica* or the "public thing." In his book, *Leading at a Higher Level*, Judge Larry Stirling introduced it this way: "The *res publica* was steely-eyed, accurate view by the Romans as to what was good for Romans. It was a strategic vision of their vast nation—its economy, its history, its icons, and most importantly, its future.

"What is *res publica*? It is an unwritten consensus that develops as a result of the collective experience. In society this is known as the collective wisdom. In the individual it is referred to as the 'emotional quotient.' It means making decisions on what is best for the long-range, overall, common good."

In other words, it was what President John F. Kennedy meant when he proclaimed: "Ask not what your country can do for you, but what you can do for your country."

FIVE: Start with simple things—new behaviors that are easy to do, and can be accomplished on an individual level without any outside intervention. One example MTS could follow would to re-examine his history of distance from the majority of child-rearing and home-keeping endeavors. True, many males today are becoming more involved, but the reality is that, in the main, they're just dipping their toes into the pool of work, responsibility, and consciousness it requires to successfully raise a family, meet their emotional and growth needs, and maintain that same level of commitment to the children once they leave the house and begin their independent lives. That's what nurturement is all about—it's a lifetime commitment, not just something one does at Thanksgiving, religious holidays, and birthdays. It's a way of life. Males need to understand that fact and restructure their paradigm accordingly.

At this point, I would like to talk about some of the new, good signs. The X-Generation male is indulging in behaviors that are a throw-back to positive examples from the past such as carrying their children like papooses and realizing the importance of this early bonding and love connection. Maternity-leave for fathers is becoming more acceptable in corporate America. We are encouraging gentler, sensitive males. Education is moving away from hard-core competition toward building, not tearing down. And finally, we find great masses of people returning to a search for spirituality and realizing such an institution acts as a type of mucilage to society—that no matter what the religion is, it represents people of good heart who wish to be more socially and community-oriented. Worldwide, humankind is beginning to accept the fact that democracy makes sense and that all people have rights—especially females. So slowly, we're encouraging each other to become more nurturing. We've seen what happened to the dinosaur and, for the moment, most of us vote "No" to following in their footsteps toward extinction. During our relatively brief stay on this planet, the flexibility of our species has been one of our most outstanding characteristics—our ability to adapt to new situations.

Another of the positive signs I see on the horizon is the Internet and its "imaging" form of communication. The idea that a picture is worth a thousand words is doing much to counter the left-brained thinking of the purely written word. The funeral for John F. Kennedy signaled the beginning of that "imaging" impact on the public consciousness, and the role of communications "imaging" has increased geometrically ever since. This phenomenon has also signaled the return of nurturing as an acceptable forum of public sharing and inspiration. Most recently we've witnessed the return of female icons to a platform of acceptance and enlightenment—the Virgin Mary, Joan of Arc, Mother Theresa, and even Princess Diana. Could it be that Goddesses will return one day soon as part of our "new" religions?

Joseph Campbell addresses this very idea in the conclusion to his Introduction to *The Language of the Goddess* by Marija Gimbutas. "One cannot but feel that in the appearance of this volume at just the turn of the century there is evident relevance to the universally recognized need in our time for a general transformation of consciousness. The message here is of an actual age of harmony and peace in accord with the creative energies of nature which for a spell of some four thousand prehistoric years anteceded the five thousand of what James Joyce has termed the 'nightmare' (of contending tribal and national interests) from which it is now certainly time for this planet to wake."

One final word. There's another reason I wrote this book; it's kind of a public confession. I now see that I was wrong in how I lived my life as a male. I now see what I missed because of what I thought I was as a man. I used to think the role for a man was to be strong, to earn money, to provide food and shelter, and to develop talents within myself and utilize them for my family. But now I look back and see things I missed because I didn't have the strong nurturing skills that females—to a greater or lesser extent— have with their children and their own gender.

I envy and admire the social sustenance women bring and receive in their relationships with each other. I don't believe males (in the main) are blessed with that ability, even though they try; I know I don't have it. I look at what females do and how they act with each other and say to myself, "Hey, this is a loss in your life, Lenny; you are unable to do what they do." So, I would say the relationship between mother and child (where the father can't be the mother) and the relationship that women have with each other are both areas where I feel a deep sense of loss within myself and for my family.

How I wish it had been otherwise.

So, with this book, I am attempting to provide an opportunity for you males who read this book to realize that you too will one day experience a deep personal loss if you continue following the same old, failed male roles of modern society. The good news is you have a choice. You're in charge. You can make a difference.

Bibliography

Balswick, Jack. *Men at the Crossroads: Beyond Traditional Roles & Modern Options*. Downers Grove, Illinois: InterVarsity Press, 1992.

Baring, Anne and Jules Cashford. *The Myth of the Goddess: Evolution of an Image*. London: Penguin Books, Ltd., 1993.

Bly, Robert. *Iron John: A Book About Men*. New York: Random House, 1992.

Bridges, John and F. David Peat. *Turbulent Mirror*. New York: Harper & Row, 1989.

Cunliffe, Barry. *Prehistoric Europe: An Illustrated History*. New York: Oxford University Press, 1997.

Eisler, Riane. *The Chalice & the Blade: Our History, Our Future*. New York: HarperCollins, 1988.

Farrell, Warren, Ph.D. *The Myth of Male Power*. New York: Simon & Schuster, 1993.

Farrell, Warren, Ph.D. *Women Can't Hear What Men Don't Say: Destroying myths, creating love*. New York: Penguin Putnam Inc, 1999.

Garbarino, James, Ph.D. *Lost Boys: Why our sons turn violent and how we can save them*. New York: The Free Press, 1999.

Ghiglieri, Michael P. *The Dark Side of Man: Tracing the origins of male violence.* Reading, Massachusetts: Perseus Books, 1999.

Gimbutas, Marija. *The Language of the Goddess.* New York: HarperCollins, 1991.

Gimbutus, Marija. *The Goddesses and Gods of Old Europe 6500-3500 BC: Myths and Cult Images.* Berkeley: University of California Press, 1982.

Keen, Sam. *Fire in the Belly: On being a man.* New York: Bantam Books, 1991.

Kindon, Dan, Ph.D., and Michael Thompson, Ph.D. *Raising Cain: Protecting the emotional life of boys.* New York: Ballantine Books, 2000.

Krishnamurti, J., PH.D., and David Bohm, Ph.D. *The Ending of Time.* New York: HarperCollins, 1985.

Parrinder, Edward Geoffery. *World Religions: From Ancient History to the Present.* New York: The Hamlyn Publishing Group, Newnes Books, 1983.

Shlain, Leonard. *The Alphabet Versus the Goddess: The Conflict Between Word and Image.* New York: Penguin Putnam Books, 1998.

Sheehy, Gail. *Understanding Men's Passages: Discovering the new map of men's lives.* New York: Random House, 1998.

Stirling, Larry. *Leading at a Higher Level: The Challenge of Good Government Through Servant Leadership.* Escondido, California: The Ken Blanchard Companies, 2000.

Sullivan, Andrew. "The HE Hormone." New York: *The New York Times Magazine*, April 2, 2000.

Summers, Christina Hoff. *The War Against Boys: How misguided feminism is harming our young men.* New York: Simon & Shuster, 2000.

Tiger, Lionel. *The Decline of Males.* New York: Golden Books, 1999.

Tucher, Andie, Ed. *Bill Moyers: A World of Ideas II.* New York: Doubleday, 1990.

Walker, Barbara G. *The Woman's Dictionary of Symbols & Sacred Objects.* New York: Harper & Row, 1988.

Index